SERENA
SEWS

First published in the UK in 2022 by
Black & White Publishing Ltd
Nautical House, 104 Commercial Street, Edinburgh EH6 6NF

A division of Bonnier Books UK
4th Floor, Victoria House, Bloomsbury Square, London, WC1B 4DA
Owned by Bonnier Books
Sveavägen 56, Stockholm, Sweden

Step-by-step photography by Serena Baker
All other photography copyright © Susie Lowe
Cover design by Richard Budd

Downloadable patterns and size chart on page 21 by Rebecca Jane Patterns

A CIP catalogue record for this book is available from the British Library.

ISBN: 978 1 78530 388 3

1 3 5 7 9 10 8 6 4 2

Design and pattern diagrams by Black & White Publishing
Printed and bound in Turkey

www.blackandwhitepublishing.com

SERENA
SEWS

How to Make Beautiful, Interchangeable,
Sustainable and Unique Clothes

SERENA BAKER

BLACK & WHITE PUBLISHING

For Granda, who we lost last year and who would have thought this was just lovely.

SAMMY McILROY
1934-2021

CONTENTS

INTRODUCTION

Hello! First, I want to say thank you for buying my book. It means so much to me that you have picked it up. Being given the opportunity to write a book about my passion has been wonderful, and I feel extremely grateful that people want to learn about sewing from me.

I started my sewing journey at fifteen. It captured me instantly and I worked towards a goal of making my own prom dress. Along the way I made some pretty suspect items of clothing, but I achieved my goal and wore that prom dress with pride! After leaving school, I had a couple of years where I sewed less; I was working, then started medical school and, unfortunately, rooms in student halls don't really take sewing space into consideration. Since then, I have been very fortunate to have space to sew throughout my student life. I am now finishing my fifth year of a six-year medical degree, and during that time have learned to fit sewing in wherever I can.

When we were in the first lockdown, I applied to be on *The Great British Sewing Bee*. I was in lockdown with my brother and his girlfriend, Sarah (who was my model for the final). During this time, series six of the show was airing and simultaneously I was applying for the next series. I vividly remember sitting on the sofa watching the final of series six with George and Sarah, and Sarah said: "Imagine if that was you in a year's time." And it was. I'm still not over it.

Competing in *The Great British Sewing Bee* changed my life. It gave me a platform to share the craft of sewing that I am so passionate about. Early in my sewing journey I was heavily inspired by the people I saw sewing on television, since, apart from Mum, they're the only people I saw doing that. It was a show I could learn from and be inspired by. I hope I can be that for other people who might want to start sewing now. Becoming part of a sewing community was one of my favourite parts of the process; it was freeing to be able to talk about sewing with people who fully understood it and weren't just listening to you to be polite about your hobby.

But my sewing isn't just about filming a television show. It has become a constant in my life that allows me space to decompress and be creative, while at the same time giving me the ability to make more sustainable fashion choices and develop skills. Writing this book has been an extension of why I love sewing – and an opportunity to share my skills and techniques with you.

From this book, I hope you get a sense of how fluid and experimental sewing can be – have fun with it! Outside of filming a television show, sewing should be fun and relaxing! Once you have the basic techniques down and feel more confident in your abilities, I hope you take inspiration from these pages and make the designs unique to you and your style, to fit them into your life. Maybe you are here to learn about upcycling/refashioning; this kind of sewing is a bit different to sewing with a plain length of fabric, but I want to show you the basic approach I take.

No matter your sewing experience, I hope that through these pages you can be inspired by design, learn about technique and experiment with style.

Some of the projects in the book have hashtags attached to them, this is to make it easier to share your projects and see what others have been creating on social media! #SerenaSews

ACCESSIBILITY IN SEWING

Sewing is expensive. I was fortunate enough to be able to use my mum's old sewing machine when I started out, but even buying the patterns, fabric and tools you need all adds up. Sewing as a teenager and then as a student means I learned to sew on a budget. I hope I can show you that you don't need endless patterns and fancy tools to sew. You can buy them all if you want, but don't feel bad or held back if you can't!

A big way I saved money was creating my own patterns by building on basic blocks instead of buying new patterns for every project. This also allowed me to develop my pattern and design skills. That is the premise of the projects within this book: every item in this book can be made from a bodice, skirt and sleeve block, an existing garment, or basic patterns I show you how to draft.

The expense of fabric is more difficult to overcome. If you are planning a more exuberant project, save up and spend that time planning the project more. I find that if I have to wait a period of time before I can start sewing, it's a bit like waiting for Christmas morning: I just get more excited about finally being able to start sewing. I speak about this more in the "Sustainability in Sewing" chapter, but often sustainable fabrics are more expensive. Don't feel guilty if you can't afford them. Buy what you can afford, and what you need. There are plenty of sources of cheaper and second-hand fabric that you can explore too: try eBay and charity shops, or purchase deadstock fabric.

WHY I LOVE SEWING

The feeling sewing gives you is unlike any other. Being able to clothe myself in garments I have crafted makes me feel powerful. I'm literally wrapped in my own love and attention. But there are other reasons why I love it, and here are a few.

ORIGINALITY & STYLE

One of the reasons I started sewing was because I wanted to explore my style more. At fifteen, I wanted to express myself through clothes and I hated feeling like the clothes I wore were just to fit in with the people around me. Sewing has helped me to feel more confident wearing clothes or even other things (mainly shoes) that other people around me wouldn't be seen dead in – shout-out to my brother who, when he saw the shoes I was wearing for the GBSB final, said, "Those are disgusting." Thanks for the support, George.

I love making clothes that make me feel happy and comfortable. I always say my style icon is Villanelle from *Killing Eve*; not only her bold and voluminous statement pieces but her everyday wardrobe too. I have taken much inspiration from her and those around me in the past few years, to experiment and learn the styles that make me feel most like me.

I want people to see how sewing allows a unique type of self-expression that has been invaluable to me. Knowing the garment you are wearing is the only one to exist in the world is an incredible feeling.

LEARNING NEW SKILLS

I love challenging myself in many aspects of my life; I have quite a competitive nature, but I am often most competitive with myself (my family may disagree after many Pictionary games). Sewing offers ample opportunity to continually develop skills and learn new ones. Sometimes this can feel overwhelming, and I recommend focussing on one new skill at a time. For example, once you know the basic skills in "Build from the Basics", you can experiment with additional design features, such as ruffles or embroidery, or trickier fabrics. Trying one new skill at a time will help you build confidence and knowledge without it feeling demoralising to not quite succeed the first time around.

Sometimes, learning new skills can be overwhelming and frustrating if you don't quite get it yet. This is normal and if you do feel frustrated, just take a break. Coming back to the task with fresh eyes can give you a new perspective.

SUSTAINABILITY

I speak on this much more in the next chapter, "Sustainability in Sewing", but I wanted to mention this as one of the reasons I love sewing. I didn't really know what "sustainability" was until a few years ago, but I've always been interested in shopping second-hand and upcycling clothes. This helped me explore new styles and discover my own, as well as learn new techniques for upcycling and refashioning clothing, as you need a very different approach compared to using new fabric. Learning how to sew more sustainably has been a focus of mine for the past couple of years, and it's what this book aims to help you achieve too.

ESCAPISM

The summer I started sewing was also the summer my parents separated. During this time, I threw myself into sewing; it was the only place where I wasn't thinking about anything else going on. I think my parents knew what was happening, but at the time I didn't twig that I was using sewing as an escape. Both they and my siblings were very considerate of my newfound passion; I took over the kitchen table for endless sewing sessions that went on easily until midnight before Dad made space for me in a spare corner of the house. And at Mum's, we would do sewing projects together, initially sharing her old sewing machine until I got my own. We would top-and-tail at the kitchen table all weekend to make our projects. My sewing machine was ferried back and forth between both parents' houses for quite a few years!

My point is, sewing has always been and continues to be that place of solace for me. Fitting sewing around my degree has taken a while to get used to, but even planning projects and looking for inspiration gives me that bit of headspace away from my degree that I need. It allows me to fully switch off, while at the same time be creative and learn new skills. You might not feel this effect straight away if you're a complete beginner, but please persevere and you might well find your own peace of mind.

HOW TO USE THIS BOOK

This book is designed to teach you the foundation skills of sewing, and to begin creating patterns from basic designs that are comfortable, versatile and will incorporate these foundational techniques. Throughout the project pages you will also come across more advanced skills, some of which are extras to add into projects; see the full list of techniques you can learn on the contents page. If you ever come across a term you don't understand and isn't explained, first refer to the glossary, and you should find out more information. At the start of each project in this book, you will find suggested fabric types to use or garments you will need. I have also listed extra items you need to complete the project; these are known as notions.

This book does not specify how much fabric you need for each project, since it depends on your pattern alterations and the exact design you want. Instead, I encourage you to create your pattern for the project and then measure how much fabric you need by laying out your fabric pieces on the floor and estimating the length of fabric required. I would advise adding a bit on for safety and remember to check the width of your fabric when measuring. Most patterns are cut out from fabric that is folded in half lengthways.

For the three pattern alteration chapters, the projects are created to build pattern alterations upon each other, so you can work through the projects in a chapter to gradually increase the difficulty and deviation from the original pattern blocks. When tackling the refashioning projects, I have taken a more liberal approach and I recommend you do too. These ones require a bit more creativity in order to cut out and fit your pattern to the garment you are refashioning, therefore they could be trickier, and you may want to tackle these once you are more confident in your sewing skills. If you want, you can do these projects from fabric first to try the techniques out.

Please, whatever happens, do not stress. If something goes wrong, know it is completely normal. Sometimes patterns take some trial and error before getting them right, so you can create toiles (essentially practice garments made from cheaper fabric and without completely finishing them) to ensure the pattern and fit is correct before cutting into nice fabric. Even during sewing, sometimes we make mistakes. I use my stitch-picker with almost every single project I sew and often have to take breaks when I get frustrated.

I want you to put your own spin on these projects, pick fabrics and designs you love and that make you feel good wearing them. That is the true power of sewing. And have fun!

Top Tip

Plan, plan, plan. I very rarely start sewing something without some sort of plan. This means preparing your pattern and sourcing your notions before starting to sew the project – otherwise you will be raring to go and realise you've run out of matching thread. Heartbreaking.

CHAPTER 1

SUSTAINABILITY IN SEWING

I'm not going to regurgitate facts at you about why we need to become more sustainable and aware of our impact in every aspect of our lives. You all know why. This is a sewing book, and that inherently means producing more clothing. For me, sewing will always be a part of my life and I am actively trying to find ways to reduce the impact of the clothes I make. This is an evolving process with plenty of learning along the way, and I want to try and share that with you. My changes include becoming more conscious of my fabric choices and taking on refashioning clothing.

Becoming more aware of these things is not the same as completely changing the way you operate overnight – this is unachievable. It is important to make changes that are sustainable to you too. For example: sustainable fabric is expensive, whereas polyester fabric is cheap, and it is okay to buy the cheaper fabric if it is what you can afford. I have used tulle fabric in this book, and it is polyester, but I don't feel guilty about this because I made the dress for a once-in-a-lifetime event and I could not afford other fabric that gave the same impact. I think we just have to stop and think about how we could personally make that garment more eco-friendly.

We can all help to create change, and I believe that my contribution is sharing how I personally try to cut down the impact of my sewing, to help others do the same while still enjoying this beautiful hobby.

SLOW SEWING

I don't make everything, but I try to make or buy second-hand where possible. Avoiding fast fashion quite literally helped me slow down my fashion consumption: suddenly I had to start thinking for myself about what I actually needed in my wardrobe, what I actually wanted to wear and if I could make it myself. You become more aware of gaps in your wardrobe, and what clothes you need to fill them. I stopped making impulsive choices about clothes or fabric that I ended up regretting.

Slowing down like this also helped me develop my personal style. When I used to buy fast fashion, I would always buy random items that didn't go together and didn't reflect me or my style. Since starting to make a conscious effort to think about what my personal style is, I've been wearing clothes that feel like me and how I want to represent myself to the world. It makes you feel more individual, especially when you've made one-of-a-kind pieces. You can also use sewing skills to help you alter second-hand items to fit you better or make simple changes.

I believe slow sewing also means spending more time on the planning aspect, creating a pattern you love and finding the right fabric, rather than jumping on an idea and buying the things you need straight away. It's a bit like buying clothes: if you see a fabric or pattern you like, take a few days and if you are still thinking about that fabric or pattern, then you probably do really love it! But if you have completely forgotten about it, chances are you weren't that bothered — it's very easy to get caught up in the moment.

Spending more time planning also ensures you can evaluate how the garment will work for you. Will you actually wear the clothes in real life? Considerations I like to make when planning garments include:

- Functionality for everyday life: this is a fancy way of saying "add pockets and make it comfortable"
- Longevity of the garment: this includes fabric type, quality of sewing and if I can still wear the garment when my body changes (using elastic is a great way to ensure this)
- Versatility: will I be able to wear this item with other garments I already own, or have I just created another gap in my wardrobe I need to fill? I also like making clothes that can span more than one season's weather; for example, tops that can be layered in winter and worn alone in summer

In my experience, taking time to design clothes that work in my life means I enjoy the sewing process and wearing them even more, hopefully for years to come. Not all garments will tick all boxes, but again, it's all about taking the time to think about these things and make

changes where possible. It's okay to make exuberant things too sometimes!

Your fabric choice can be a deciding factor on the impact of your clothes. Sustainable fabrics are becoming more available and cheaper. Each fabric has pros and cons; for example, cotton seems like a good sustainable choice but actually takes a huge amount of water to produce. Researching fabric types suitable to your project will help you make decisions, keeping a budget and all of those factors above in mind.

One way I love getting around the fabric choice issue is by using fabric in existing garments, which I like to call refashioning!

REFASHIONING

WHAT IS REFASHIONING?

Ditching fast fashion helped me stream-line my wardrobe and style, and gave me more focus with my sewing. It also helped me explore a whole new aspect of sewing — refashioning. I tend to think of refashioning as changing the structure of a garment to make a whole new garment, whereas upcycling is where you make some alterations, but the base structure stays the same. At the end of the day, we are turning unloved second-hand items into new stylish garments that will be loved again.

I really got into refashioning during the first lockdown of the pandemic. This was because I had a lot more time to sew but not a lot more money to buy fabric. I was at a stage in my life where I still had a lot of clothes from my teens that didn't fit me anymore but that I was hanging on to just in case they did again. I got over that quickly and since charity shops were closed, I tried refashioning them. Some of the items I had bought new and some I had sewn myself, but I always used ones that I loved the fabric of or had a special/fun detail.

APPROACH TO REFASHIONING

In this book I will be using items that you can find quite easily second-hand, but after you try these projects, why not experiment with other unique items you might find in a local charity shop? Look for items with a detail you love and can use in a new design, like a big ruffle or some cute embroidery. You might not have a set idea for your project when you buy the item, but you can build an idea around a feature of the garment. This could even be the fact that it's floaty fabric, or it has ruching, or it has some buttons somewhere — literally anything goes.

There are no set rules for refashioning (or sewing for that matter), and I cannot emphasise enough that it is all about trial and error. I do that constantly, go back and forth on ideas and try out new techniques. It's completely normal and I love this process because you are forced to come up with new ways to troubleshoot problems.

Sometimes I find it useful to go shopping with an idea for a project so that I can try and focus on buying a specific type of clothing suitable for that project. Other times the item of clothing I am refashioning is a random piece from my own wardrobe or one handed down to me — and in these cases I must get a bit more creative to fit the project around the garment. This approach was more

difficult to get used to for me as I love having everything planned out, but once I was a bit more experienced in it, I found it freeing to sew that way.

Refashioning is also a great time to try out new skills to incorporate into sewing — you could try hand embroidery, machine embroidery, pattern draping, dyeing, printing . . . the list goes on. Get experimenting — have fun — and remember you don't have 90 minutes to do this challenge, so take your time.

A NOTE ON BUYING SECOND-HAND CLOTHES

Accessibility is a problem in the fashion industry and often plus-sized clothes have less variety available. This issue prevails into second-hand clothing too, with sources having fewer plus-sized clothes available to buy. It would be easy, as a slimmer person, to buy larger clothes for access to the greater amount of fabric, but this is not the approach to take. All refashioning/upcycling projects in this book are done using clothing sizes that I wear (for men's clothing I used a small/medium), meaning that the projects can be completed by anyone of any size using clothing of that size.

SCRAPS

An easy way to reduce the impact of your sewing is to become more aware of your scraps and use them for other projects. The accessories in this book are all made from scraps of fabrics, and only need very small remnants; that way your accessories can match the clothes you make. And even the teeny, tiniest scraps can be used as stuffing!

CHAPTER 2

ALWAYS BE ORGANISED

ESSENTIAL TOOLKIT

Sewing is not the most accessible hobby because of the number of tools it requires. Many of these you may have in the house anyway or may be able to borrow from someone. When I first started sewing, I used my mum's old machine for eighteen months before I was able to get my own. Not everyone is as lucky to have access to a machine, but you can buy beginner machines for around £80-£100. Maybe you could even split the cost with a friend, if you are both up for trying it out!

When starting out, gather the basic tools you need and then you can build up as you progress with your sewing.

Top Tip

Invest in good fabric scissors. I'm not the kind of sewist to have a room full of sewing tools, but many are worth investing in and good fabric scissors are a must for precise sewing. Plus, the noise when they cut cleanly through fabric is incredibly satisfying.

- ☐ Sewing machine – remember to check the guidebook for oiling instructions, you should really do this after every 8 hours of stitching, and get machine services every 2-3 years
- ☐ Iron and ironing board
- ☐ Fabric scissors
- ☐ Small embroidery scissors – for snipping threads and clipping seams
- ☐ Stitch-picker – for small mistakes we make. I use mine all the time
- ☐ Sewing machine needles – see "Build from the Basics" (page 29) for choosing the right needle size
- ☐ Hand-sewing needle
- ☐ Thread – try and buy good quality thread, as it does make a difference. Polyester thread is the strongest, while cotton thread has a tendency to snap under pressure, so keep that in mind when choosing thread for a project.
- ☐ Pins – nice and sharp
- ☐ Ruler – I still use the ruler I had in my school pencil case. If it measures, it works.
- ☐ Measuring tape
- ☐ Tailor's chalk/fabric pen
- ☐ Pen for pattern drafting
- ☐ Paper for pattern drafting – either pattern paper, brown paper or sometimes I even use wrapping paper
- ☐ Safety pins – for inserting elastic
- ☐ Spare bobbins

OPTIONAL TOOLS

There are endless sewing tools out there, designed to aid you with every step of a project. For storage and price reasons, I tend to stick to the essentials plus a few extra tools I find useful. Feel free to go mad and buy all of the tools you can find, but if you are feeling less extravagant, here are a few I find worth the price.

Mannequin: the cheaper versions of these are "standard sizes", so like anything else that is "standard size" they will never be the same as your body. Mine has a shorter torso, smaller waist, and bigger boobs than me (oh, funny that), but it is still useful for drafting and displaying garments. The more expensive ones are adjustable, so they will be more representative of your body and can be adjusted as your body changes.

Quilting ruler: essentially a longer and wider ruler that is useful for pattern drafting and making bias tape.

Tailor's ham: very useful for pressing curved seams, such as armholes.

Rolled hem foot: an attachment for your sewing machine that helps you sew teeny tiny hems. This saves a ridiculous amount of time, especially in projects with massive hems, which you will definitely encounter in this book.

Tube turner: helps you turn tubes to the right side. I had one of these, but it wasn't very sturdy, and it broke pretty quickly. If you are buying one, try and find a good-quality one. Now, I just use a needle and thread to turn tubes. See "Build from the Basics" (page 48) for a step-by-step guide!

Pinking shears: these are useful scissors to finish seams if you don't have, or don't want to invest in, an overlocker .

Overlocker foot: an attachment for your sewing machine that you can use to finish seams.

Overlocker: another kind of machine that is great for finishing seams.

Top Tip

Focus your mind and try not to be distracted. I find that setting aside time dedicated to sewing, whether that is 20 minutes or 4 hours, makes me instantly enjoy and engage with the sewing process more. This allows my brain to switch off from other responsibilities as I know this is "sewing time" and I can concentrate on that. Being focussed doesn't necessarily mean you are working in silence; get some music on, and enjoy yourself, just allow yourself to switch off from other activities.

SEWING ORGANISATION

As a student, I am extremely fortunate to have the space to sew; it is small, but I love it and am grateful for my sewing corner. Before I came to uni, I sewed on the dining table in my mum's or dad's house – having to shuffle my machine between the two houses and move my sewing off the table when we needed to eat. It was quite social, really, but I'm not sure my family appreciated the sound of the overlocker going all weekend. Oops. I dream of a day when I can have a room in my house dedicated to sewing, it will happen!

My sewing spaces in the past and present mean I've always kept my sewing supplies as minimal as possible and over the years I have learned how to streamline my sewing to fit into the space I have. Here are some tips to staying organised and tidy with sewing if you are working with a communal or small space.

FABRIC STORAGE

If you are short on space, I recommend buying fabric as you need for a project rather than buying fabric and then finding a project for it. This will prevent you having a big, space-consuming fabric stash and will help you save money. I think this way of buying fabric is also a bit more sustainable, as you are only buying what you need rather than buying impulsively. Use up remnants and scraps to prevent fabric build-up or sell remnants on.

PATTERN STORAGE

In the past year I finally took time to organise my patterns and it has made such a difference to how tidy my sewing space is. I don't tend to buy a huge number of patterns, preferring to draft/make alterations to bodice blocks where possible to create my designs, but sometimes you just need a trustworthy pattern. Over time, they build up and, without a proper system, mine became an unorganised, chaotic mess. Now I have a system that I can use whenever I buy/make a new pattern to sustain the organisation.

When you create new patterns from the blocks in this book, I recommend doing it on thin paper and filing every new pattern into folders labelled with the pattern and size they are.

SEWING SPACE

A tidy and organised sewing space has always allowed me to be more creative. Maybe this is just the way my brain works, but when my workspace is tidy, so is my brain space. As a general rule, I have a sewing space tidy-up after I finish every project. This means I can start a new project with a fresh mind and fresh-looking space. Put things back in their place after you have finished using them, hoover up loose threads and just generally try to tidy up after every project.

One simple tip that changed my sewing space was to have a spare mug/cup next to my sewing machine, and every time I cut loose threads from a project, I put them in the mug. This stops the loose threads from being strewn about your sewing space, and instead you can just put the mug contents into the bin after every project.

Even if your space is small, you can still decorate it with nice bits and bobs too! Display some pictures, or store threads in a glass jar for a splash of colour.

GET READY FOR YOUR NEXT PROJECT

Sewing takes a surprisingly large amount of preparation time. The bits before actually getting started sewing can be a bit tedious, but I recommend being organised with them so that when you start sewing you can just get on with it and not have to worry about whether you have everything you need! This means:

- Have your pattern ready: cut out, draft or alter your pattern to create your new one in preparation.
- Pre-wash your fabric: sometimes fabric shrinks when it is washed for the first time. To avoid spending hours on a project, washing it and ending up with a warped garment – pre-wash. This means washing the length of fabric at a temperature you would use if washing the finished garment, and it ensures any fabric shrinking happens before you cut pattern pieces out. Give your pre-washed fabric an iron, and you're ready to start cutting.
- Check your notions list: these are things other than fabric that you will need for the project. Gathering everything you need before you start will save you having to run to the shop for more thread mid-hem.
- Cut out your pieces: this is the part of sewing I hate most, so I like getting it out of the way as soon as possible. Some people even bulk cut projects – spend a few hours cutting out multiple projects so you can enjoy sewing without having to worry about cutting out!
- Set aside some time to fully focus on the project.

CHAPTER 3

PREPARE YOUR PATTERNS

Sometimes it can be difficult to understand patterns, especially as a beginner, so this chapter aims to explain pattern sizes, symbols and adjustments. After working through this chapter, you will have a bodice, sleeve and skirt pattern that fits you and that you can use to create clothes in the coming chapters.

Many projects in this book have a forgiving fit, so they don't need to fit your body curve for curve as they are looser or have details that make them have a slightly adjustable fit. This is to make it a bit easier to fit for beginners and also because I love wearing comfortable clothes!

I recommend measuring yourself and tracing the blocks as per the size guide. Make any adjustments you need to the basic blocks and re-draw your final patterns. Then, sew a toile (a practice garment) from these to check the fit and make any further adjustments necessary. Once you are happy with the fit, you have a basic bodice and sleeve block, and you can continue with the book projects.

DOWNLOADING THE PATTERNS

With this book you have been given access to a bodice, a sleeve and an A-line skirt block. These are all you require to create the projects in the upcoming pages. To access them, follow the QR code below or type the link into a browser and you will be able to download the files.

www.blackandwhitepublishing.com/pages/serena-sews-block-patterns

Note: if you already have basic pattern blocks that you love and fit you well, then feel free to use these when making the projects. The garments will still turn out great!

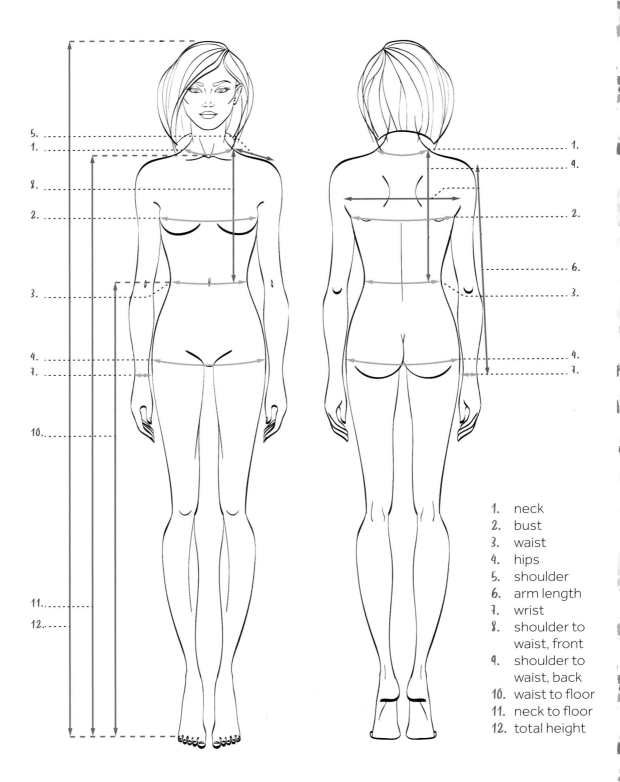

1. neck
2. bust
3. waist
4. hips
5. shoulder
6. arm length
7. wrist
8. shoulder to
   waist, front
9. shoulder to
   waist, back
10. waist to floor
11. neck to floor
12. total height

MEASURING YOURSELF

Sewing patterns are just like standard-size clothes – they're made for a "standard body", which doesn't exist. This means that to get a good fit, we need to understand our own measurements and adjust the pattern blocks to create one fitted for our own bodies. On the left are the basic measurements we need in order to adjust the basic blocks, but during the projects you will be asked to take more to make further adjustments.

SIZE GUIDE

Please see the UK size chart below to find out which pattern guide to use. A more detailed chart – plus EU, US and AU sizes – is available with the downloadable pattern guide. See page 19 for information on how to download.

These measurements are in reference to the finished garment. All measurements are in centimetres.

SIZE	BUST	WAIST	HIPS	SHOULDER LENGTH	SHOULDER TO HEM (BODICE)	SKIRT LENGH	FULL SLEEVE LENGTH
6	87	86.6	103.2	10.8	41	53.8	52
8	91.6	90.6	105.2	11.3	41.7	55	53
10	94.8	94.4	107.2	11.5	42.5	56	54
12	98.6	98.6	109.2	11.7	43.3	57	55
14	102.8	102.8	111.2	11.8	44	58	56
16	106	106.6	113.2	11.9	44.7	59	57
18	111	110.2	115.2	12.1	45.5	60	58
20	114.8	113.8	117.2	12.2	46.4	61	59
22	119	116.4	119.2	12.4	47	62	60

Bust: around the widest part of chest (across your nipples) and sitting flat across your back (2)

Waist: around your natural waist (3)

Hips: around the widest part of hips (4)

Shoulder: neck to shoulder (5)

Front bodice length: neck to waist over bust (8)

Back bodice length: nape of neck to waist (9)

Sleeve length: shoulder to wrist (6)

Wrist: around wrist (7)

READING PATTERNS

At first glance, sewing patterns look like a very complicated mess of lines and symbols. Here is a list of the common symbols you will encounter during this book and what they mean.

MULTI-SIZE CUTTING LINE

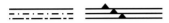

Patterns that are printed with multiple sizes on one sheet will look like this. Sometimes the lines can overlap and become a bit confusing. Before cutting out, I recommend finding your size (see page 21 for sizing and grading on page 24) and using a colourful pen or highlighter to draw around the pattern piece. Then follow the coloured line when cutting out – this makes it much easier.

STITCHING LINE

- - - - - - - - - - - - -

This tends to only be drawn on patterns printed in a single size. This is where your stitching will be.

LENGTHEN/SHORTEN LINES

Lines you will use to add or remove length from a pattern piece. See section below for instructions on how to do this. If the pattern doesn't have these, you will need to draw one on. These should be perpendicular to the grainline (see paragraph to right) and sit below the bust on the bodice, and at the bicep and forearm of the sleeve pattern.

NOTCHES

Markings that help the pieces of fabric fit together perfectly. When cutting out, mark the notch with a small triangle, or make a small mark with chalk. If there are two small lines or a wider shape, mark with two chalk marks or an elongated triangle so you can differentiate the notches when sewing.

MARKINGS TO TRANSFER

Again, this helps to ensure your pieces will fit together nicely and are typically used on trickier seams to sew, e.g., armholes. Mark these with chalk or a tailor's tack – a very loose hand stitch that can be removed after sewing the seam.

GATHERING LINES

This wiggly line indicates where the fabric of this piece will be gathered during the project. Typically seen on waistlines of skirts, or armholes of puffy sleeves.

FOLD LINES

This marking indicates that when cutting your fabric, this piece should be placed on the fold of the grainline, resulting in cutting out one fabric piece that is double that of the pattern piece.

GRAINLINES

This marking indicates how to place the pattern piece on the fabric. The arrow should follow the grainline of the fabric. See section "Build from the Basics" (page 29) to learn more about what a grainline is.

DARTS

See section "Build from the Basics" (page 29) to learn a bit more about what darts are and how to sew them. This is how they will be represented on patterns. When cutting out, mark the two base points and top point of the dart with chalk.

TOP TIPS FOR PATTERN MAKING

HAVE A SYSTEM

When altering and drafting patterns, things can get messy quickly. Try and have a pattern organisation system in place to help you stay tidy and organised in your sewing space. Label all of your patterns with the name and size of the pattern plus any adjustments you made.

TRACE YOUR BLOCKS

Once you have a bodice and sleeve block that fits you well, don't draw on it or cut into it. When you want to use it for a project, trace a copy of it (including all markings) and work from that one. This ensures you never lose or damage your blocks!

MAKE NOTES

Write down every single measurement you take and every single pattern alteration you make. Trust me, just do it. You will find that sometimes a seemingly insignificant measurement you took suddenly becomes quite important. But even if you don't end up using them all, it's still useful to have a note of them.

CUTTING PATTERNS

When cutting your pattern, you might have to grade between sizes; for example, I am usually a UK size 10 at the bust and hips but 12 at the waist. To grade between sizes, draw a curved line to join the pattern lines at bust, waist and hip lines of the size you want. See examples below for how to grade.

Make sure when you are cutting the pattern to follow all pattern markings present.

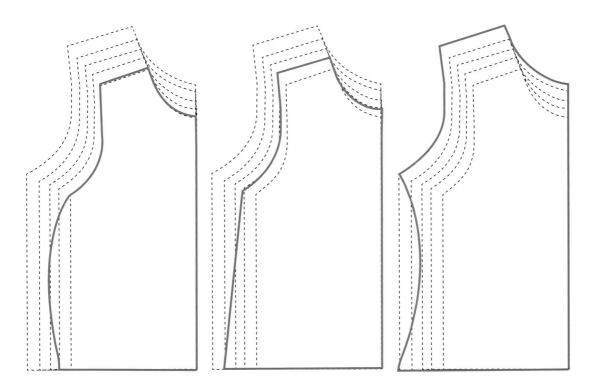

Top Tip

When cutting out, have your fabric lying flat and folded along the long edge. This is standard for patterns and allows you to cut two pattern pieces on the fold as required. Try to cut out on flat surfaces without movement; rugs and carpets are harder to cut out on and might not give you as precise lines.

ALTERING PATTERNS

On the page to the right you will find basic pattern adjustments you can make to your blocks, so you have a bodice and sleeve block personalised for your body. Once you make an adjustment, sew a toile to check the fit before making others.

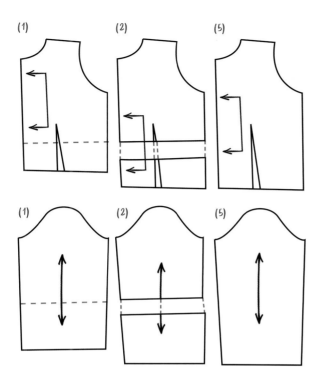

ADDING BODICE AND SLEEVE LENGTH

1. Cut along lengthen/shorten line
2. Separate pieces evenly to desired measurement
3. Place piece of paper underneath pieces and secure paper down
4. Draw new pattern lines to join edges evenly
5. Trace new pattern piece and remember to copy all markings

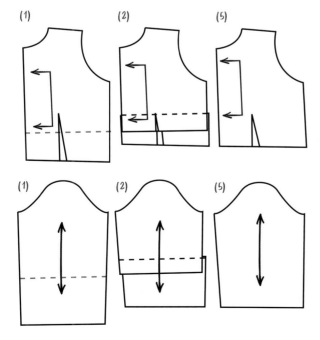

REMOVING BODICE AND SLEEVE LENGTH

1. Cut along lengthen/shorten line
2. Separate pieces evenly and overlap to desired measurement
3. Place piece of paper underneath pieces and secure paper down
4. Draw new pattern lines to join edges evenly
5. Trace new pattern piece and remember to copy all markings

ADJUSTING DARTS

Dart adjustments will be necessary if the bust point of your bodice has to be moved; for example, moving darts down for a lower bust, or up for a higher bust.

ADDING LENGTH TO A DART
1. Directly above dart point, measure how much you want to add on to length and draw a new dart point
2. Join new dart point to dart base to create new sides

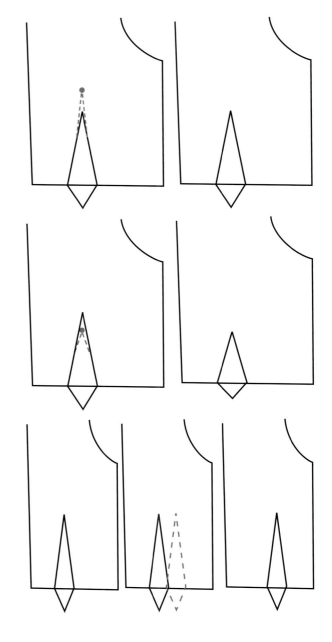

REMOVING LENGTH FROM A DART
1. Directly below dart point, measure how much you want to remove from the length and draw a new dart point
2. Join new dart point to dart base to create new sides

MOVING A DART
1. Redraw dart point by measuring how much you want to move the dart and draw a new dart point
2. Move base points of dart by same measurement
3. Rejoin dart points to base
4. Move the triangle underneath the dart to maintain original shape of bodice

FULL OR SMALL BUST ADJUSTMENT

These are slightly more complex adjustments and for this I recommend you find content from an experienced pattern maker. I have never used these adjustments and so it would be unfair (and quite frankly plagiarism) to copy content from online into my book. There are plenty of instructions out there for you to follow!

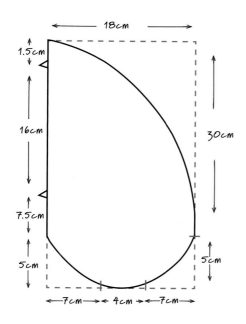

DRAFTING POCKETS

IN-SEAM POCKETS

In-seam pockets are a great skill to learn. To make them, you will need to cut out four of the same shape and if your fabric has a right and wrong side, make sure there are two mirrored pairs. The notches on the pattern piece are used to help form the pocket opening, so don't miss them out!

Here is a diagram to help you draft your own (it already includes 1.5cm seam allowances).

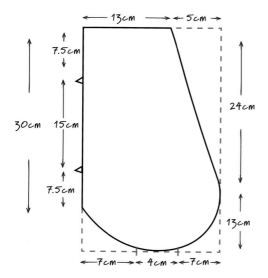

WAIST-SEAM POCKETS

Waist-seam pockets are secured into the waistband of a garment. When making them, you will need to cut out four of the same shape, and if your fabric has a right and wrong side, make sure there are two mirrored pairs. The notches on the pattern piece are used to help form the pocket opening, so don't miss them out!

Here is a diagram to help you draft your own (it already includes 1.5cm seam allowances).

CHAPTER 4

BUILD FROM THE BASICS

The following techniques represent the foundation skills of sewing. You can make hundreds of projects with these skills alone. If you are a beginner, I would recommend practising the skills before using them in a project – I didn't do this when I started out and I really messed up some nice projects because of my impatience. You can also experiment with some of these techniques to add detail to your garments!

The images in this chapter have contrasting thread to demonstrate the stitching lines. When you are using these skills in a project remember to use matching thread!

PRINCIPLES

FABRIC – TYPE AND WEIGHT

There are so many types of fabrics made in a myriad of ways. You could lose yourself down a rabbit hole researching them. The way fabrics are made and the impact this has on the environment is really interesting, but not something I will discuss here. I'm not nearly knowledgeable enough on the topic to write about it.

What I will discuss with you is the type of fabric you will use in this book. This is non-stretch, woven fabric such as cotton. These come in a range of weights and

prices – cotton lawns have a finer weave and are lightweight, but also tend to be more expensive. Cotton poplins are slightly heavier and cheaper and cotton drill is heavier still. Cotton can be mixed with polyester to produce cheaper fabrics.

Woven fabrics have important properties you must keep in mind when cutting out. They are created with warp and weft threads that are threaded over and under each other to create a woven structure. The finished edges of the fabric at either side are known as the selvage and the width is usually 112cm (for crafting cotton) or 150cm (for dress fabric). You then buy the fabric by the length needed.

The thread running parallel to the selvage creates a grainline while the perpendicular thread creates a cross grain. Grainlines are essential to know about as patterns will have a grainline arrow you need to line up with the fabric grain. The diagonal of the fabric is called the bias, and this can stretch, which is a useful feature (see page 40 on making bias binding) but can also warp the shape of pattern pieces. Lining up the grainline of the pattern piece and fabric ensures the garment will sit on your body correctly when completed.

In this book, when making pattern adjustments, keep the grainline of the pattern pieces the same unless I specify otherwise.

The machine needle size you choose will depend on your fabric weight. Lightweight fabrics need a smaller needle, e.g. size 70. Midweight fabrics need a size 80 (most common for this book) and heavyweight fabrics a size 90 or 100 if very heavy. Trial the needle size on a scrap of fabric to make sure it will sew nicely.

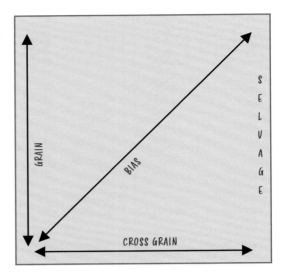

EXAMPLES OF FABRIC OF DIFFERENT WEIGHTS

Lightweight fabric: viscose, chiffon, georgette, cotton lawn

Midweight fabric: cotton, velvet, cotton sateen

Heavy fabric: denim, corduroy, canvas, wool

Top Tip

Learn skills on stable fabric, for example cotton, before moving to tricky textiles. This lets you focus on learning the skill without worrying about other technicalities such as the fabric sliding all over the place or getting caught in your machine. Once you have the foundation skills, I recommend experimenting with trickier fabrics.

BASIC STITCHES

There are only three stitches you will be asked to use during this book.

Unless you are finishing seams, the stitch used throughout the book is a straight stitch.

For each seam, you must backstitch at the beginning and end of each seam to secure the stitches. Backstitching means sewing forward a few stitches, back a few and then forward to continue on with the seam. Repeat this at each end of the seam.

SEAM ALLOWANCES

If asked to finish a seam, see section below.

In the book you may be asked to trim or clip seam allowances.

Straight stitch: most basic stitch on your machine.

Zigzag: typically used for stretchy fabrics, but since those are not being used in this book, you will only use a zigzag stitch for finishing seams (see section below).

Overlock stitch: potentially used for finishing seams (see section below).

Trimming: to cut the seam allowance down to a few mm to reduce bulk.

Clipping: is used on curves to ensure they maintain the right shape when the garment is completed. Clipping means cuts are made in the seam allowance without cutting through the stitches themselves.

Trimming and clipping on an outer curve: if the seam is on the outside of a curve you will need to cut triangles into the seam allowance, so bulk is reduced when turned the right way.

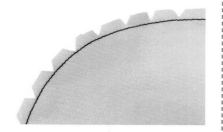

Trimming and clipping on an inner curve: if the seam is on the inside of a curve, cuts need to be made in the seam allowance, so it can lie flat when turned the right way.

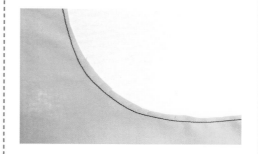

INTERFACING

Interfacing is used to stiffen sections of fabric that need a bit more weight or structure. It is typically used on facings, belts or ties. Once you have attached the interfacing to the fabric, you can treat this combination as one piece and continue with the project.

There are three things to consider when buying interfacing:

1. Weight of your fabric
2. Interfacing weave
3. Method for applying interfacing

If in doubt, buy interfacing from a sewing shop and ask someone for a bit of help picking one that suits your fabric. Remember to take a sample of your fabric along so they can feel it.

WEIGHT

When buying interfacing, you need to buy interfacing of a similar weight to your fabric. See fabric section above for more info on fabric weight.

WEAVE

There are three types of interfacing based on the way it is produced. The patterns in this book all use non-stretch fabric, and the best type of interfacing to buy is woven or non-woven rather than knit. I would recommend using non-woven interfacing for ease of cutting out.

Woven: this interfacing has a grainline, just like fabric, so you will need to note this when cutting your pieces out. Woven interfacing does not stretch

Non-woven: this interfacing does not have a grainline, so can be cut in any direction without fraying. Non-woven interfacing does not stretch

Knit: used for stretchy fabrics.

Top Tip

I recommend learning one new skill at a time. In this book I have used the skills in projects you might be learning for the first time. It will be easier to choose projects with fewer new skills to start with and build from there. Focussing on one new skill makes things seem less overwhelming to beginner sewists.

METHOD FOR APPLYING INTERFACING

There are two different types of interfacing, based on how they are combined with the fabric.

Iron-on interfacing: does what it says on the tin. This interfacing has glue on one side of it that is melted by the heat of the iron. This permanently fuses it to your fabric. This should be suitable for any garments/fabrics you use in this book.

Iron the interfacing onto the wrong side of the fabric using a dry heat – the highest your fabric can take. Cover the interfacing with muslin or spare cloth while ironing to prevent it sticking to the iron.

Sew-in interfacing: for sew-on interfacing, you will baste the interfacing to your fabric pieces just inside the seam allowance (a bit like stay stitching, see below). Continue with pattern as normal.

This interfacing is useful for fabrics you cannot iron, or for when you don't necessarily want an extremely stiff piece of fabric.

STAY STITCHING

Stay stitching is used to secure curved edges of fabric before sewing them. Curved edges have sections where the fabric is cut on the bias and is therefore prone to stretching out. Stay stitching is typically used on necklines and armholes. To stay stitch an edge, sew around the whole edge just within your seam allowance for that edge. For example, if you are stay stitching a neckline and the neckline will be sewn onto a facing with a 1.5cm seam allowance, stay stitch at 1.2cm from edge of fabric. The stay stitching will not be visible in the final garment.

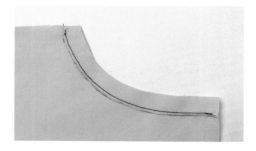

Black pen line: 1.5cm seam allowance line
Black thread: 1.2cm stay stitching line

UNDERSTITCHING

Understitching is used to help seams fall where they are supposed to and stay inside garments. They are classically used on neckline facings, pocket bags/facings and armhole facings. Understitching keeps the seam allowance from rolling to the outside of the garment. The stitching will not be visible from the outside of the garment but use matching thread anyway.

STEPS

1. Sew seam with right sides of fabric together
2. Trim and clip seam allowance as needed
3. Press seam towards inside of garment
4. Stitch 2-3mm away from seam on the facing, catching the seam allowance in this stitching
5. Press facing (or whatever else you are sewing) to the inside of the garment

You can also choose to topstitch this edge to ensure the facing doesn't roll to the outside even more. (See page 35.)

(1)

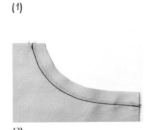

(2)

(3)

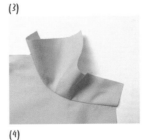

(4)

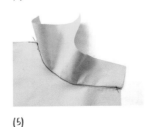

(5)

TOPSTITCHING

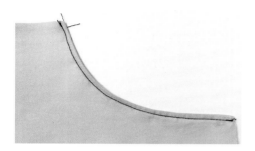

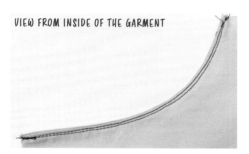

VIEW FROM INSIDE OF THE GARMENT

Topstitching has a few uses: it can be decorative, for example contrast topstitching on jeans, or ensure lining and facing pieces stay on the inside of the garment. It is sewn on completed seams. Stitch 2–3mm away from edge of fabric/seam the whole way around. You can use an edge stitching foot (machine attachment) to help you keep this measurement straight or follow markings on your machine.

You can get creative with topstitching: use it to create extra designs on your items for uniqueness, like I did with these wide-leg jeans!

SEWING DARTS

Darts are triangles sewn into garments to create 3D shapes from 2D pieces of fabric – since our bodies are in fact 3D! They are very easy to sew and are usually one of the first steps in a project. The position and depth of darts can be easily adjusted to fit your body.

(1)

(2)

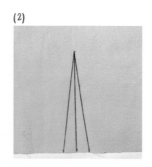

(3)

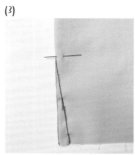

(4)

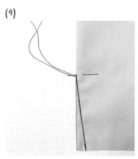

(5)

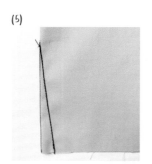

(6)

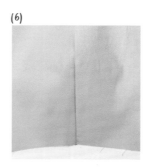

STEPS

1. On the wrong side of fabric, following the pattern, mark the base and point of dart triangle
2. Join the base and point with chalk/pen to create triangle
3. Fold dart along middle line and pin along the outside lines of triangle. Mark the point of dart with a horizontal pin. You can baste along this line with hand stitches if you want to
4. Sew from fabric edge towards point, following the chalk line. When nearing the point, use your hand to feed the machine for the last few stitches and make sure the last stitch is right on the edge of the point. Do not backstitch at point of dart. Cut threads of point with about 10cm of thread remaining
5. Tie the loose threads at the point in three secure knots. Cut threads close to knot
6. Press dart flat. Remove basting stitches if you need to

GATHERING

Gathering is used to add volume to a garment, commonly at the waist seam to create a voluminous skirt. For the gathering stitches, ensure you use polyester thread because cotton thread will snap under the pressure of gathering. This technique is used lots during this book!

To create gathers you need a length of fabric that is 1.5–2x the length of the piece you will be sewing on to. I find that gathering a piece twice the length gives the nicest and fullest look for most garments.

You can experiment with gathering to add into various parts of a garment, or to create a tiered skirt like the dress on page 88, or add ruffles onto tops, sleeves or anywhere you like!

STEPS

1. Set your machine to the longest stitch length and thread with contrasting thread colour
2. Sew two rows of parallel stitches along edge that will be gathered, either side of the seam allowance, e.g. if seam allowance is 1.5cm, stitch a row at 1cm and one at 2cm. Do not backstitch these rows. The white chalk line (white dotted line in photo) is the seam allowance marking
3. At one end of the rows tie the two top threads and trim about 1cm above knot
4. At the other end, tie the two bottom threads and trim about 1cm above knot

(2)

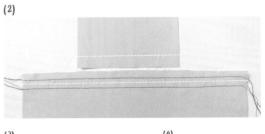

(3)

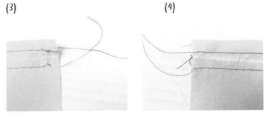

(4)

5. Use pins to mark halfway and quarter ways along the fabric edge to be gathered – do the same along the edge it will be sewn to
6. Use the loose threads left at either edge to gather the fabric down the length required
7. Pin the fabric edges right sides together at halfway and quarter-way marks
8. Even out the gathers between these marks and pin the remaining fabric down

9. Put the right-coloured thread in the machine and set stitch length to normal
10. Sew the seam at normal seam allowance, making backstitches at either end to secure
11. Remove two rows of gathering stitches
12. Finish seam, for example by overlocking
13. Press seam away from gathers

(5)

(6)

(8)

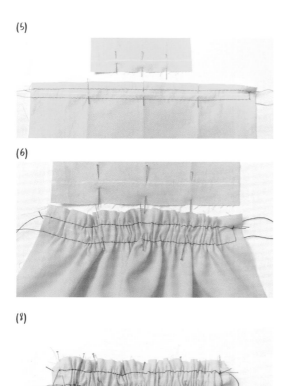

(10)

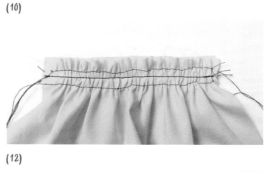

(12)

(13)

BIAS BINDING

You will notice with fabrics such as cotton (non-stretch) that if you pull the fabric along the grain or cross grain it will not stretch, but if you pull it along the bias, the fabric stretches slightly. Bias binding (also called bias tape) is made from strips of fabric cut on the diagonal of a fabric. Because the bias has some stretch, these strips can mould around curved edges and sit nice and flat, e.g. around a neckline or armhole.

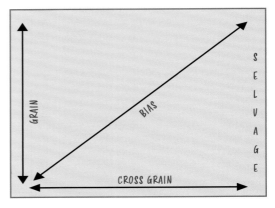

You can either buy or make bias binding – making it means the bias binding will match your project perfectly, but sometimes people like to add a contrasting bias for a bit of detail. It's easy to make and is also a great use of weirdly shaped scraps – stitch them all together to make a big length of bias binding you can use for another project!

MAKING BIAS BINDING

1. Mark the bias line on your fabric using chalk
2. Make 4cm wide lines parallel to this for as much length as you need for your project
3. Cut this using sharp scissors to get a neat line
4. Iron each long edge of bias binding towards the middle of the strip.
5. Iron this in half

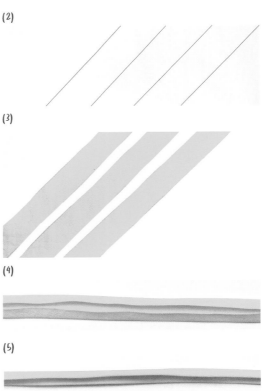

(2)

(3)

(4)

(5)

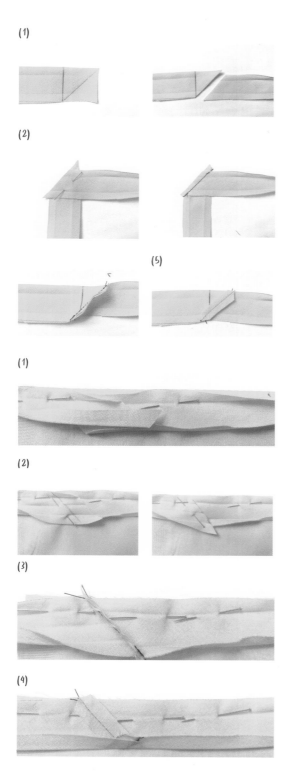

(1)

(2)

(5)

(1)

(2)

(3)

(4)

SEWING STRIPS

You may need to join shorter strips to create a strip of bias binding long enough for your project.

1. Cut diagonal lines across the ends of your strips by drawing a square and a diagonal line within this
2. Place the strips right sides together along this diagonal line, overlapping the points by 1cm
3. Sew the diagonal line at 1cm
4. Press seam open
5. Cut points off
6. Continue as normal making bias tape

SEWING INTO LOOP

In this book you will need to sew bias binding into a loop to complete edges, such as a neckline or armhole.

1. Pin bias binding all the way around edge, overlapping bias edges by a few centimetres
2. Cut any excess fabric off the top layer of binding so that the top layer over-laps the bottom by 2cm, ensuring the diagonal lines point the same way
3. Sew the binding into a loop (following above instructions)
4. Press the seam flat and the folds back into the binding
5. Sew the binding down as normal now (see following section)

SEWING BIAS BINDING METHOD 1

This method leaves the finished edge without visible binding and removes 1cm allowance from the edge.

1. Open the bias binding and pin along the opening – right sides together. You might need to stretch the binding slightly as you do this so it fits onto the curve nicely
2. Stitch along the first fold you made in the bias binding at 1cm
3. Trim and clip this seam
4. Understitch this seam towards the binding
5. Fold the bias binding along the middle fold; this should conceal the seam
6. Press this flat
7. Fold the binding inside the opening, pin
8. Stitch close to the edge of the bias binding
9. Press flat

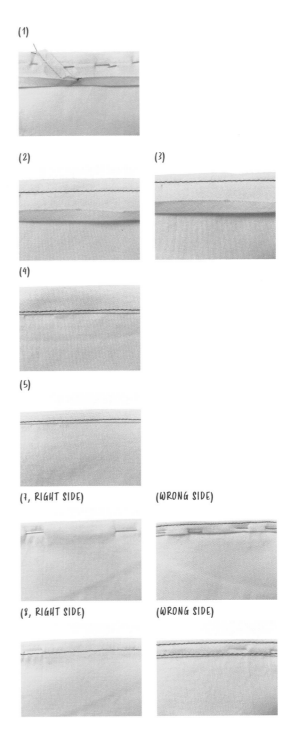

(1)

(2)   (3)

(4)

(5)

(7, RIGHT SIDE)   (WRONG SIDE)

(8, RIGHT SIDE)   (WRONG SIDE)

(1)

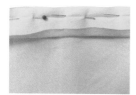

(2)

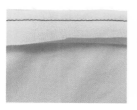

(3)

(4)

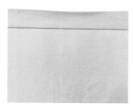

(6)

SEWING BIAS BINDING METHOD 2

This method leaves the finished edge with visible binding and does not remove any allowance from the edge.

1. Open the bias binding and pin along the opening – right sides together. You might need to stretch the binding slightly as you do this, so it fits onto the curve nicely
2. Stitch along the first fold you made in the bias binding at 1cm
3. Trim and clip this seam
4. Press seam allowance towards binding
5. Fold the bias binding along the middle fold; this should conceal the seam. Press as you fold
6. Pin and stitch close to the edge of the bias binding (at about 8mm from edge)
7. Press binding flat

HAND SEWING

Sometimes the projects in this book call for a little hand sewing to finish off techniques neatly. Generally, I prefer doing as much on the machine as I can because it is more secure and will withstand washing better, but sometimes hand stitching is unavoidable. You will need to learn basic hand sewing skills such as stitching buttons on or other notions such as a hook and eye. You can also choose to hand stitch hems if you prefer to not have visible stitching from the outside of the garment.

When I do hand sewing I prefer to double back the thread, so I am sewing with two strands – I just think this is stronger. I don't do this for blind hems (see page 47 for blind hem instructions).

Hand sewing is easy – you just use the needle to pick up a bit of fabric from one side and then do the same for the other side. This is called a slip stitch. (See page 47 for instructions.) When you reach the end of your sewing, make sure to do a few stitches and a knot to make the stitches secure.

BASTING STITCHES

These are optional for you to use during the book to secure seams or darts before you stitch them on your machine. It means you don't have to focus on removing pins at the same time as sewing. Basting stitches are also called running stitches and are easy peasy. Thread a needle with either a single or double length, knot the end and thread the needle in and out of the fabric to create long stitches of about 1cm length. You don't need to reinforce them in any way. When you reach the end, you can do a wee knot to secure that too. Remove the basting stitches after properly sewing that seam.

BUTTONS

Buttons only appear in this book as an additional feature from refashioned garments. They are a great opportunity to add detail and style to a garment; for example, in one of the refashioned projects from men's shirts I change the buttons to add extra detail and make them a bit more exciting than the small white buttons you typically get with men's shirts. I love looking in charity shops for old buttons: you can often find some cool ones and for about 1p each.

Sew buttons on using hand stitching. Mark using a pen or chalk where you want the button to go. Stitch the button on using a double thread for strength and be sure to tie knots at the end of the thread to secure it. If the button has four holes, you can cross the threads for detail.

FINISHING SEAMS

There are a few different ways you can finish your seams. For these projects we will be finishing the edges of our seams and pressing them flat. It is vitally important to finish the edges of your project so it can withstand washing many times without raw edges fraying.

TO FINISH THE EDGE, YOU CAN EITHER:

Use pinking shears – most likely to eventually fray in the wash

Zigzag stitch the edges using a sewing machine – you can do this on any sewing machine

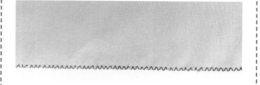

Overlock stitch the edge using a sewing machine – you can buy a foot for most domestic sewing machines that have this function

Use an overlocker to finish the edge – requires an overlocker machine, but offers much faster and secure stitches

Fancier seams such as French seams and bias-bound seams, but they won't be used in this book

HEMMING

Hems finish the bottom edges of fabric, for example on trousers, skirts and sleeves. There are a few different types of hems you can choose to do. In this book, I mostly leave the type of hem used unspecified so that you can choose your preferred method. Just remember when creating the patterns to add enough hem allowance onto your project.

SINGLE-TURNED HEM

1. Finish the edge of the hem
2. Turn up by hem allowance and press this flat
3. Pin around the edge and stitch down close to turned edge, either with machine or hand stitching (see blind hem)

DOUBLE-TURNED HEM

This technique fully encloses the edge of the hem. When using this technique, make sure you add enough hem allowance onto the pattern before cutting out, as it uses more fabric than a single turn.

1. Press the hem upwards by first turn allowance (usually small, e.g. 1cm)
2. Press up again by second turn allowance (either the same or bigger, e.g. 2.5cm)
3. Pin and stitch close to turned edge

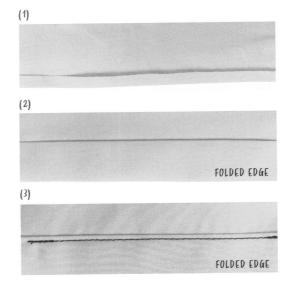

(3)

(5)

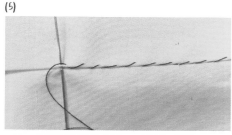

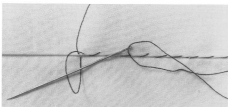

(INSIDE)   (OUTSIDE)

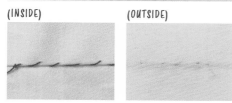

BLIND HEM

This is done using hand stitching or with a special foot attachment for your machine (I have never used this, so you're on your own there).

FOR HAND STITCHING

1. Start with pressed hem
2. Thread the needle with a single thread and tie a knot at the end
3. When stitching, carefully pick up only one fibre of the section that will be visible and then a few from the hemmed edge
4. Continue making stitches an even distance apart all around the hem
5. Secure with a few stitches in only the hem allowance, not outer fabric . This means these stitches won't be visible from the outside. When sewing the last securing stitches, create a knot using the loop of thread to further secure the thread
6. Cut thread close to knot
7. Press hem

The hem can either be a single turn with a finished edge, or a double turn. Make sure to press either before stitching down.

ROLLED HEM

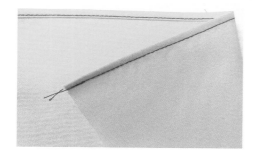

This technique is very useful for fine fabric and long hems (which you will encounter in this book). It uses a rolled hem foot attachment for your sewing machine. Follow the instructions on the foot packet. This technique is very fiddly at first but once you get the hang of it, it can save lots of time when adding ruffles and gathers – plus the finished look is an extremely neat, thin hem that looks great.

TURNING TUBES

Some of the projects in the book require you to turn tubes from inside out to the right side. You can buy tools to help with this, but I find them flimsy and not very good. Instead, I prefer using a simple needle and thread (use polyester thread for this):

1. Thread your needle and double back the thread until it is about the length of the tube, then tie a knot in the end
2. Sew a couple of stitches into the end of the tube
3. Thread the needle into the tube, blunt end first
4. Pull the needle through and the tube will start to turn in on itself
5. Gently ease the tube through; don't tug too hard on the thread or it could snap
6. When the tube is turned to the right way, cut the threads off and press tube flat

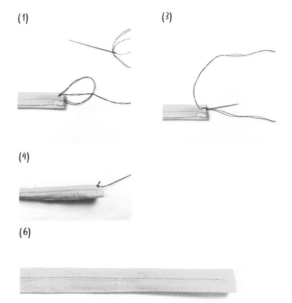

(1)

(3)

(4)

(6)

CREATING TIES WITH POINTS

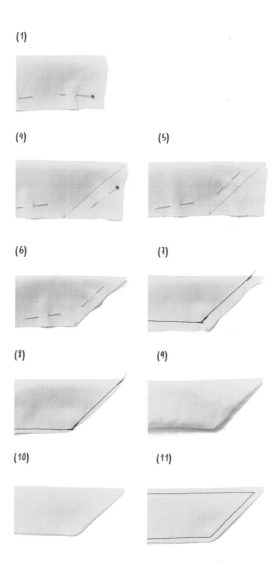

(1)

(4)   (5)

(6)   (7)

(8)   (9)

(10)   (11)

In this book, you will be creating ties a few times, and I enjoy adding points to the end sometimes. You can add one pointy end for ties, or two pointy ends for a belt. This is really easy to do to any width of tie, and this is how:

1. Fold the rectangle right sides together along the long edge
2. Note the width measurement of the folded rectangle along the short end; for example, mine is 4cm
3. Along the long edge, mark in the measurement from previous step; mine is 4cm
4. Join this new mark to the corner of the folded edge to create a diagonal line
5. Pin this line through both layers to keep in place
6. Cut through the diagonal line.
7. Sew along long edge and diagonal line with seam allowance as indicated, adding backstitches at the corners to reinforce
8. Trim and clip seam allowances, removing almost all seam allowance at the corner and point
9. Turn right sides out, using a pin or needle and thread to help you get a pointy point
10. Press flat
11. Optional – you can topstitch if you want to!

CHAPTER 5

DROP SHOULDER
PATTERN ALTERATION

Our first pattern alteration is a dropped shoulder. This means the armhole seam no longer sits right on the edge of the shoulder, but lower down on the arm. Dropping the shoulder seam is a great way to get a more relaxed fit, and also makes sewing the arms into the armhole easier as the sleeve cap is not so high with excess fabric to ease in.

This pattern alteration has endless possibilities for many projects, and I've exemplified a few here for you. I've used three projects to map the progression of pattern alterations, showing simple steps for altering the pattern slightly each time. So, we start with a simple crop top and are ending with a dress with pleat detail!

These projects are great ones to make from second-hand clothes – especially the first two as you can easily get the fabric from a men's shirt, and the button placket can be incorporated into the design as a meaningful feature. You can also make any of these from fabric instead of clothing. If you are using fabric, I advise using a light to mid-weight non-stretch fabric such as cotton lawn or poplin.

Patterns needed: bodice and sleeve blocks

Techniques learned: bias binding, gathering, pleat

Seam allowances: 1.5cm unless otherwise stated

MAKING THE PATTERN

FRONT BODICE

1. Extend shoulder seam by 5cm at sleeve end (you can make this measurement larger or smaller depending on how "dropped" you want the shoulder to be)
2. Lower armhole by 5cm at underarm
3. Widen side seam by 1.5cm
4. Create new armhole curve
5. Remove 1cm around neck edge
6. Extend neck edge by 4cm at centre front edge to mirror that of back bodice. Alter this according to step 5
7. Do not mark darts onto new bodice piece

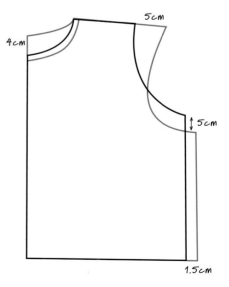

BACK BODICE

1. Extend shoulder seam by 5cm at sleeve end (you can make this measurement larger or smaller depending on how "dropped" you want the shoulder to be)
2. Lower armhole by 5cm at underarm
3. Widen side seam by 1.5cm
4. Create new armhole curve
5. Remove 1.5cm at centre back (since this pattern piece will now be on the fold)
6. Draw fold line on centre back
7. Remove 1cm around neck edge
8. Do not mark darts onto new bodice piece

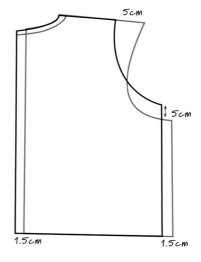

SLEEVE

1. At shoulder seam notch, reduce height by 5cm (you can make this measurement larger or smaller depending on how "dropped" you want the shoulder to be)
2. Extend side seams by 1.5cm at armhole, grading to 5cm at cuff

These changes make a basic drop shoulder bodice. To create our projects, we will be altering them slightly again.

Black: original bodice
Red: new adjustments for drop shoulder

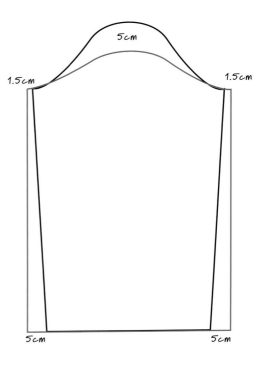

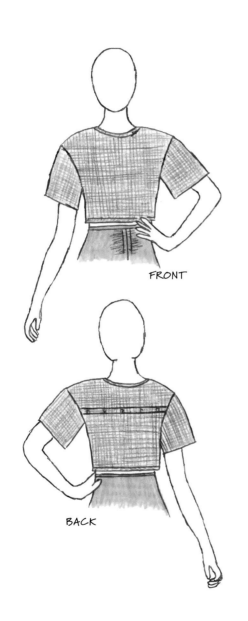

FRONT

BACK

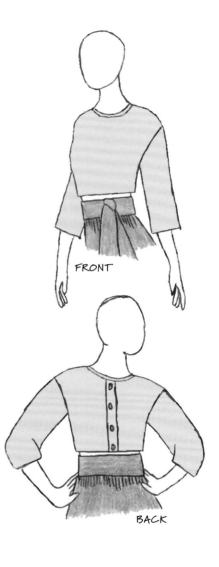

FRONT

BACK

REFASHION
REFASHION
SIMPLE CROP TOP

This crop top is extremely versatile, comfortable, and a great first project for beginners! You can play around with the sleeve length and placement of button placket to get a design you love.

For this top you will need to source a men's shirt – these can easily be found in second-hand places, e.g. charity shops. Choose the garment carefully, picking one with a colour or pattern you love. I chose a pink shirt and a gingham shirt since I knew they would fit right into my wardrobe.

NOTION LIST:
* Matching thread
* Bias tape – or make your own from instructions in "Build from the Basics" (page 40)

PATTERN PIECES

Use pattern pieces from pages 52-53; we will now add some extra alterations.

☐ 1x front on fold
* I removed 2.5cm from the bodice length to make the top cropped

☐ 1x back on fold
* I removed 2.5cm from the bodice length to make the top cropped

☐ 2x sleeve
* The length of the sleeve you will have depends on the shirt you have available
* My short sleeve length: underarm seam to hem of sleeve (unsewn) = 20.5cm
* My ¾ sleeve length: underarm seam to hem of sleeve (unsewn) = 39.5cm

☐ 1x bias binding for neckline

See pattern summary on page 58

HERE I AM WEARING THE ¾ LENGTH
SLEEVE VERSION MADE FROM A MEN'S SHIRT.

CUTTING OUT

Use the body of the shirt to cut out your front and back piece. I placed the button placket at the back of my top – you can either do this vertically or horizontally. This may depend on the size of shirt you have available. You can play around with the location of the button placket.

Use the original shirt sleeves to cut out your sleeve pattern. A good tip is using the existing sleeve seam in your garment so you can save fabric and don't have to sew another seam. If you are doing this, remember to fold back the seam allowance of the sleeve piece, and the order of sewing is slightly different: sew the side seam of the body before sewing the arms into the garment.

You will also need to create bias binding from the remaining fabric scraps from the shirt. Measure the length of the neck opening (add the front and back together) to get a vague idea of how long your bias binding needs to be – make a little extra so you don't run out. See "Build from the Basics" (page 40) to learn how to make bias binding.

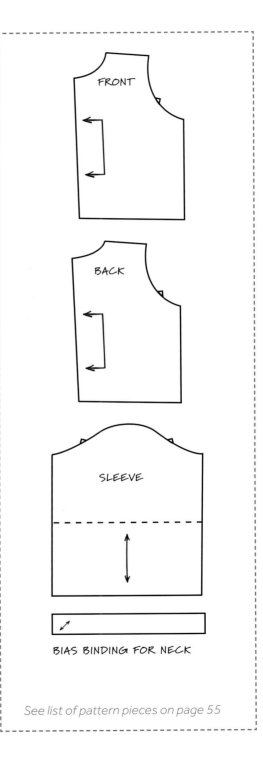

FRONT

BACK

SLEEVE

BIAS BINDING FOR NECK

See list of pattern pieces on page 55

SEWING THE TOP

1. Place front and back bodice right sides together and pin at shoulder seams
2. Sew shoulder seams and finish seam allowance, press open
3. Place sleeves and bodice right sides together at armhole and pin around armhole
4. Sew armhole seam and finish seam together – press seam allowance towards sleeve
5. Pin side seams of arms and bodice with right sides of top together
6. Sew side seams and finish seam allowance, press open
7. Hem bottom edge of top
8. Hem sleeves

I recommend stay stitching the neckline at this point and trying the top on, otherwise you risk not being able to pull the top over your head! If you can't get the top on, cut 1cm away from whole neckline and try again, keep going until it fits over your head.

9. Stitch bias binding around neckline either so it is visible or hidden – See "Build from the Basics" (page 40)
10. I chose to change the existing buttons on the pink shirt for cute tortoiseshell ones that add more detail!

When sewing my gingham version, I did not have enough fabric in the original shirt and my top ended up being shorter than I wanted. To avoid hemming the top and removing even more length, I chose to add bias binding around the bottom edge in place of a hem – this also added a nice detail since the gingham pattern was diagonal on the neck and hem edge, which stood out against the rest of the top!

GATHERED TOP

MAKING THE PATTERN

This project requires an additional pattern alteration. We will be making a horizontal seam across the body of the top, above the bust line. You can choose to add this onto the front AND back of the garment, or only the back. This will partly depend on how much fabric you have available in the item you are refashioning.

Note: if you are not using a men's shirt like me and using the button placket on this seam you will need to add seam allowance to the top portion of this seam – add 1.5cm and follow separate instructions for this seam in step 3.

NOTION LIST:
- Matching thread
- Bias tape – or make your own from instructions in "Build from the Basics" (page 40)

Draw a line where you want the seam to go, cut pattern there and add 1.5cm seam allowance to the lower side of new seam. This is because we will be cutting the top section of this seam (yoke) from the button placket on the shirt and will not need seam allowance.

The bottom section will need volume added to it, so eventually it can be gathered down. The volume you can add depends on what item of clothing you are refashioning. I added 1.5x the length of the original seam. I repeated this process for the front and back of the top.

You could also add this seam under the bust line, or at the waist, for different final looks. You could also add more tiers to the top, or even make it a dress!

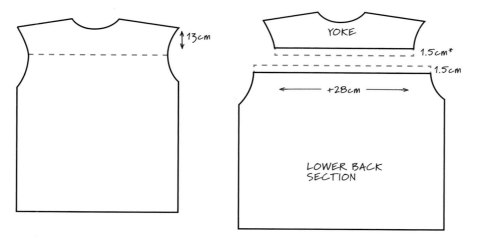

↕13cm

YOKE

1.5cm*

1.5cm

+28cm

LOWER BACK
SECTION

* add 1.5cm to yoke side of new seam if you are not
using a men's shirt like i am

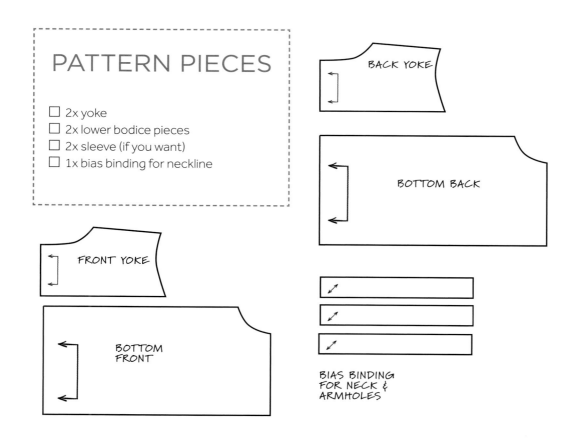

PATTERN PIECES

☐ 2x yoke
☐ 2x lower bodice pieces
☐ 2x sleeve (if you want)
☐ 1x bias binding for neckline

BACK YOKE

BOTTOM BACK

FRONT YOKE

BOTTOM
FRONT

BIAS BINDING
FOR NECK &
ARMHOLES

SEWING THE TOP

(3)

(4)

(5)

(7)

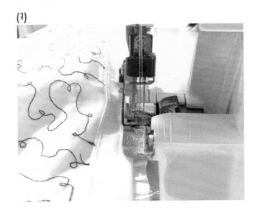

1. Stay stitch necklines and armholes
2. Cut lower sections from the back of the shirt and sleeves. You may need to sew pieces together to get enough fabric and that's okay, I did! Finish and press all seams flat
3. Gather down the lower section to the same length as the top yoke
4. Place the lower section underneath the top section, overlapping by 1.5cm (the seam allowance) so that the wrong side of the top yoke touches the right side of the lower section. You can use the gathering stitches as a guide

> *Note:* if you are not using a shirt and have added seam allowance onto both edges of this seam, stitch together (right sides together), finish and press upwards. Skip to step 9.

5. Pin along the whole length of this seam.
6. Topstitch the seam 2mm from the yoke edge
7. Finish the edge of the lower section, being careful not to cut the yoke
8. Topstitch again on the yoke, 7mm away from seam, so secure the seam allowance down
9. Press this seam
10. Sew shoulder seams right sides together and finish, press open

Sew sleeves into armhole here if you are adding sleeves, finish seam allowance and press towards sleeve right sides together

11. Sew side seams and finish, press open
12. Hem bottom edge

I recommend stay stitching the neckline at this point and trying the top on, otherwise you risk not being able to pull the top over your head! If you can't get the top on, cut 1cm away from whole neckline and try again, keep going until it fits over your head.

13. Stitch bias binding around neckline either so it is visible or hidden – see "Build from the Basics" (page 40)
14. Stitch bias binding around armholes (or add sleeves after step 10, and then carry out steps 11–13 and hem sleeves)

A LITTLE MORE

I took this project one step further by making it into a tiered dress with ruffle sleeves. All you have to do is add an extra rectangle layer onto the top pattern and add sleeve ruffles. Test yourself to create this without any more instructions! Hint: the instructions on gathering in "Build From the Basics" (page 29) should help.

MACHINE EMBROIDERY

Machine embroidery is a fun way to add extra detail and personalisation to an item of clothing. It is easy to do and requires a couple of extra tools: a darning foot attachment for your machine and an embroidery hoop.

I recommend practising this technique before you use it on your garment for the project, as it can be a bit tricky to get accustomed to using a machine in this way.

Before I did the embroidery on this shirt, I marked the yoke pieces with chalk, so I knew where to start and end my design. You will need to move the hoop along the shirt as you progress.

1. Place the fabric that you want to embroider into the hoop, so that the fabric will sit flat against a surface.
2. Prepare your machine by lowering the feed dogs, placing your darning foot on and reducing stitch length to 0.
3. Place your fabric under the machine, with right side up
4. Start stitching by doing a few stitches in the same place to secure, while holding onto the loose threads
5. Start moving the hoop gently to create your design, while trying to keep the machine at the same speed so your stitches are even lengths
6. When you have finished a section, do a few more stitches in the same spot to secure

You can get creative with the designs you make. My favourite is to add this loopy floral design, which I also used on another refashioning project I completed during the first lockdown (see photo on previous page). For this one, I embroidered all over the shirt before cutting out so that the top was covered in the embroidery and almost looked like a new fabric.

(1)

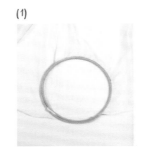

(2)

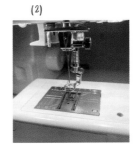

(3)

(6)

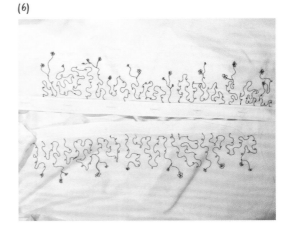

T-SHIRT DRESS

FIRST THINGS FIRST

The last project in this chapter using the dropped shoulder is for a short voluminous dress. I have also given instructions on replacing gathering with an inverted box pleat, for a more structured look. You could make this dress as long or as short as you want and could even add side seam pockets (see instructions on page 27 for side seam pockets). I didn't add pockets because my fabric was a little see-through, so you would notice them too much.

I love this style of voluminous T-shirt dress. It has big art teacher vibes, and it is the ultimate comfort outfit, plus would be a great cover up for beach days in summer.

NOTION LIST:
- Matching thread
- Bias tape – or make your own from instructions in "Build from the Basics" (page 40)

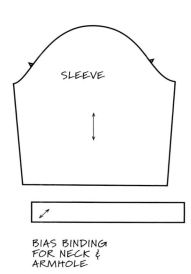

SLEEVE

BIAS BINDING
FOR NECK &
ARMHOLE

FRONT DRESS

BACK YOKE

BOTTOM BACK
DRESS

PATTERN PIECES

☐ 1x front dress – this is the original drop shoulder front bodice pattern, with length added so the side seams measured 70cm
☐ 2x yoke – see instructions on page 74
☐ 1x lower bodice dress – see instructions on page 74
☐ 2x sleeve – use the original drop shoulder sleeves. These can be any length you want, play around with the length and look of the sleeves, I went for short sleeves here, but it would also look great with ¾ length, or even add volume at the hem and elastic to create a puff sleeve look.
☐ 1x bias binding for neckline

MAKING THE PATTERN

ALTERING THE BACK BODICE PATTERN

1. Take the original back drop shoulder bodice and lengthen it so the side seams measure 70cm
2. Create a seam along the top of the pattern piece, above the bust line. Mine was 13cm down from where the shoulder seam meets the armhole
3. Add seam allowance onto either side of this new seam
4. For the bottom section, add volume to the width; I added 28cm

You could either gather the lower back section, or you could add a pleat like I did. This creates a cleaner look and is great for cotton fabrics that iron nicely like this lime green one.

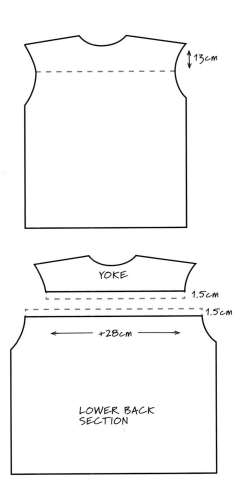

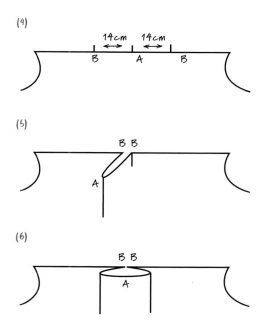

1. I created an inverted box pleat by first noting how much excess fabric was on the longer side (28cm for me)
2. Divide this by two to get your A-B measurement (14cm for me)
3. Place a pin halfway along the long edge; this is A
4. Measure along from either side of this and place more pins; this is B
5. Bring your B points together and pin this
6. Bring point A to meet B and fold the new pleat along the seam. Pin along the pleat and baste in place

SEWING THE DRESS

1. Stay stitch necklines
2. Either gather or pleat bottom back section
3. Sew yoke on using burrito method (see page 77)
4. Sew sleeves in right sides together and finish seam together – press towards sleeve
5. Sew side seams right sides together and finish, press open
6. Hem sleeves

I recommend stay stitching the neckline at this point and trying the top on, otherwise you risk not being able to pull the top over your head! If you can't get the top on, cut 1cm away from whole neckline and try again, keep going until it fits over your head.

7. Stitch bias binding around neckline either so it is visible or hidden – see "Build from the Basics" (page 40)
8. Try the dress on to make sure it is the length you desire and hem bottom edge

(1)

(2)

(3)

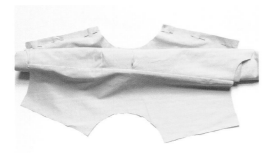

(4)

BURRITO METHOD

Sandwich the lower back piece between both yoke pieces along the straight seam, with the right side of the yoke pieces touching the lower back section. Sew this seam and trim seam allowance. Press seam flat with the yoke pressed away from the lower back piece. Place this back piece on the floor right side facing upwards (1)

Place the front dress piece onto the back dress right sides together. Pin the shoulder seam of the front dress and top yoke layer together. You can baste this seam together if you prefer but I just stuck to pinning. Fold the lower yoke downwards to get it out of the way (2)

Roll up the back and front of the dress until you can see the lower yoke (3)

Pin the lower yoke onto the already pinned shoulder seam, with right side of the lower yoke facing right side of the back dress. This will form a parcel with the dress pieces inside of it (where the name burrito method comes from!) (4)

Stitch the shoulder seam and trim seam allowance (5)

Pull the dress carefully to the right side and you will have completely enclosed shoulder seams (6)

Press shoulder seams and dress (it may get a bit crumpled during this process) (7)

CHAPTER 6
SQUARE NECK
PATTERN ALTERATION

The second big pattern alteration I will be showing you how to create is a square neckline. I have paired this with either thin straps or puffy sleeves, for summery looks. The basic adjustment to turn the bodice block into a square neckline is very simple, but with each project I will show you how to take the design further, ending with a babydoll dress that has a full skirt and ruffle sleeves.

All of these projects contain ties or shirred sections (shirring essentially turns a piece of non-stretch fabric into stretchy fabric). This means the garments you create will be comfortable to wear even with bloating or weight change and can last even longer in your wardrobe. The shirred sections are more suitable if you want to wear a bra with the garment but keep it hidden.

Pairing a square neckline with puffy sleeves is a look that has been around for the past few summers. This pattern pairing can be used to make items with a milkmaid style, but also chicer garments. There is huge scope in these patterns for individual style to flourish and to create unique items from previously loved clothing. If you choose to sew with fabric, use a light to mid-weight non-stretch one such as cotton lawn or poplin.

FRONT

BACK

REFASHION

TIE BACK CROP TOP

This crop top is a versatile and comfortable style due to the tie back feature. For the project you will need a garment made of mid-weight fabric, and if you want to add ruffles to the sleeves you could use the lining or a scrap of fabric you already have. I used an embroidered mini skirt that had lining in the original garment.

Techniques learned: gathering

Seam allowances: 1.5cm unless otherwise stated

NOTION LIST:
- Matching thread
- Bias binding – or make your own from instructions in "Build from the Basics" (page 40)

PATTERN PIECES

- ☐ 1x front (as fold)
- ☐ 2x side back
- ☐ 2x big ties (6cm wide x 45cm long)
- ☐ 2x smaller ties (3.5cm wide x 23cm long)
- ☐ 2x strap
  - 6cm wide x 42cm long (my finished strap length was 36cm long, but it is always better to create long straps that you can shorten since you can't do it the other way around!)
- ☐ 2x strap ruffle
  - 9cm wide x 55cm long (you can make this longer to create more voluminous ruffles, or a bit shorter if you are running out of fabric)
- ☐ 1x bias binding

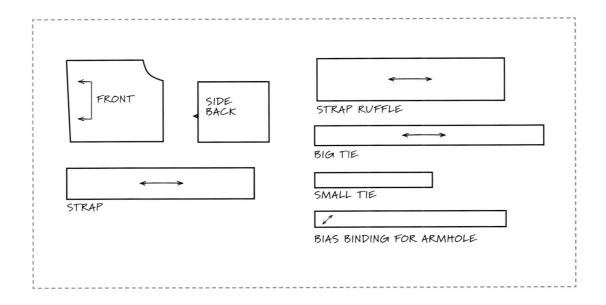

CUTTING OUT

I cut my bodice pieces from the bottom of the skirt, so that I could utilise the existing hem.

I used the rest of the outer skirt fabric to create the strap and tie pattern pieces – I needed to sew lengths of fabric together to get pieces long enough, but that's fine! The lining of my skirt was used to cut the ruffle pieces.

If you are going to hem your top, you need to add 1.5cm hem allowance onto both the front and back pattern pieces.

MAKING THE PATTERN

FRONT

1. Measure 5cm towards centre of front bodice, at level of the lowest armhole notch, and mark a point A
2. From this point, create a new armhole curve
3. Draw a line perpendicular to centre front to meet point A – this is our new front neckline
4. Add 1.5cm to top of front neckline
5. Remove 10cm of length from bodice to make cropped (omit this step if you prefer a waist-length top). See cutting out section (page 82) for guidance on the hem
6. I chose to remove the darts from the bodice for this project so the top was looser on my body, but you can keep them if you prefer

SIDE BACK

1. Draw a perpendicular line from centre back to meet the top of the side seam
2. Add 1.5cm to top of back neckline
3. Remove 6.5cm from centre back seam (you can remove more or less depending on how open you want the back of the top to be)
4. Remove 10cm of length from bodice to make cropped (you can omit this step if you prefer a waist-length top) See cutting out section for guidance on hem
5. I chose to remove the darts from the bodice for this project so the top was looser on my body, but you can keep them if you prefer

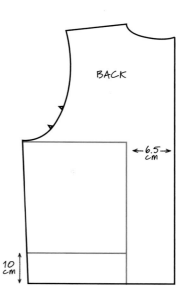

SEWING THE TOP

PREPARING THE BODICE

1. Sew darts into bodice if you are keeping them
2. Sew front and back bodice right sides together along side seams, finish seams and press open

SEWING THE BACK TIES

3. Create ties by pressing one short edge in by 1cm (we only need to finish one short edge of the ties)
4. Fold each long edge in by 1cm
5. Fold in half along long edge and pin
6. Topstitch along long edge and short edge that is finished
7. Pin ties onto edge of back bodice, right sides together, 1.5cm down from top edge
8. Sew these on with normal seam allowance of 1.5cm
9. Create smaller ties using same method and stitch these on near bottom of back seam
10. Fold this edge in by 1.5cm and stitch down at 1.2cm. Reinforce ties by stitching them down at the edge of the back bodice

SEWING THE STRAPS

11. Prepare strap ruffles by hemming one long edge and both short edges
12. Gather ruffle down to length of strap minus 1.5cm seam allowance at either end

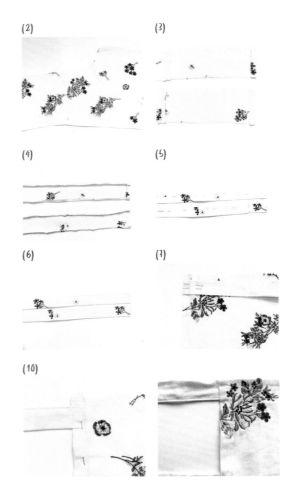

13. Create straps by pressing in half along long edge and pressing one long edge in by 1cm

Note: if you are not adding a ruffle, press both long edges in by 1cm, then press in half along long edge. Topstitch close to folded edge and you have completed straps

(15)

(16)

(17)

(18)

(19)

14. At this point, pin your straps to your bodice to check the length of them. Trim any excess strap away, making sure to account for the 1.5cm seam allowance at either end of the strap. Once length is correct, unpin from bodice, and continue creating the finished straps

If you are not making a ruffle, skip to step 18

15. On the unfolded long edge of strap, sew gathered ruffle right sides together on with 1cm seam allowance, leaving 1.5cm free at either end of strap. Press this seam away from ruffle
16. Fold strap along middle fold you created earlier and pin in place. Any raw seams should now be hidden
17. Topstitch along edge of strap to finish
18. Pin straps to bodice right sides together, with ruffles facing towards the armhole. Leave 1cm at front bodice armhole and 8cm from back of bodice. Stitch down with 1.5cm seam allowance at front neck edge, and 1cm on bodice back

COMPLETING THE TOP

19. Finish top edges of bodice and fold inwards by 1.5cm. Stitch at 1.2cm to secure
20. Finish edges of armhole with bias binding technique (see page 40) with hidden binding, folding short end of binding in by 1cm at either end to hide raw edges
21. Hem the bottom edge if you need to

THE
CHIC DRESS

FIRST THINGS FIRST

I designed this dress to attend my cousin's wedding. They decided to have the wedding outside, which could have been very hit or miss for England, but fortunately it was a hit! The sunniest weekend of the summer fell on the weekend of their wedding, which was great for me because I love heat and was wearing a flowy dress; not so lucky for those wearing suits. My dress ended up being the perfect thing for a heatwave.

The tie back and elasticated waist section make it loose and comfortable, plus easy to put on without any other closures. I also added adjustable straps using hardware typically seen in lingerie making, which makes the dress easier to fit and adds detail. Play around with the number and length of the tiers to create a completely different look or use a cotton fabric to form a wider silhouette. If you want to, you could also add in waist seam pockets! See "Prepare your Patterns" (page 28) for instructions. My fabric was too thin and would be weighed down by any pockets, so I chose not to.

I picked out these fabrics with some sewing friends in my favourite fabric shop in Glasgow (where I have many happy memories of fabric shopping with my mum back in the day). Thank you to Jen and Ben for helping me pick colours that complement each other so well! Take some time to consider the colours you want to use in your dress and think about which one you want next to your face. The colours could either have a flow, like mine, or be completely contrasting for a different look. You will need to buy the same fabric in different colours.

Patterns needed: bodice block

Techniques learned: darts, bagging out, adjustable straps

Seam allowances: 1.5cm unless otherwise stated

NOTION LIST:
- Matching thread
- Rings and sliders – 1cm wide
- 1cm wide elastic: you will need approximately 1/6th of your waist measurement, but it is cheap, so buy more and make sure you have enough

MAKING THE PATTERN

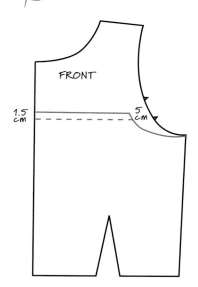

FRONT BODICE & LINING

1. Measure 5cm towards centre of front bodice, at level of the lowest armhole notch, and mark a point A
2. From this point, create a new armhole curve
3. Draw a line perpendicular to centre front to meet point A – this is our new front neckline
4. Add 1.5cm to top of front neckline
5. If you want your dress waistline to sit above your natural waist, you can remove length from the bodice

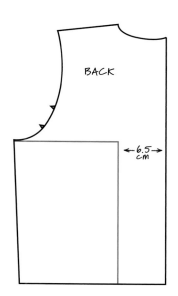

SIDE BACK BODICE & LINING

1. Draw a perpendicular line from centre back to meet the top of the side seam
2. Remove 6.5cm from centre back seam (you can remove more or less depending on how open you want the back of the top to be)
3. If you want your dress waistline to sit above your natural waist, you can remove length from the bodice
4. I removed the darts from the back of the bodice to create a looser style, but you can keep them if you want a closer fit

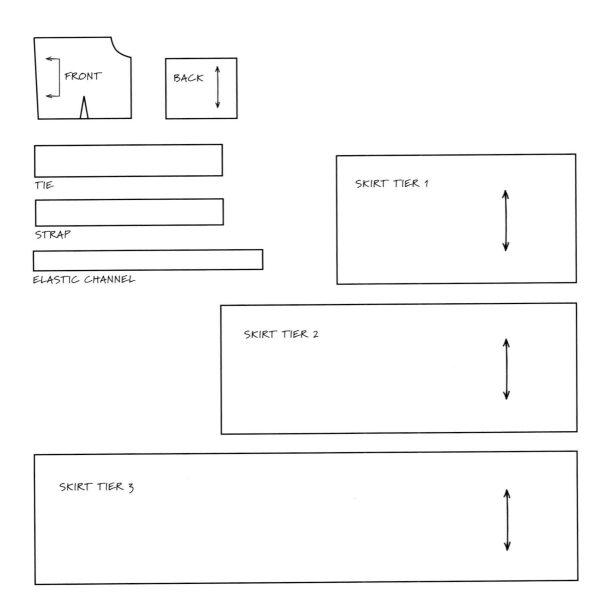

ELASTIC CHANNEL

- Length is dependent on your waist measurement
- Cut from fabric of top tier of skirt

A NOTE ON THE SKIRT

I chose to make my skirt full length and split it into three tiers of even length. You can experiment with different numbers and lengths of tiers or create dresses that are shorter or a bit longer. Have fun with it! My total finished skirt length is 93cm from waist to hem. The following measurements are my personal ones (including all seam allowances), but yours may differ due to tier lengths and waist measurement.

As the tiers get wider, you will need to piece fabric together to create a section long enough. Make sure you account for this when buying the fabric you need for the project.

PATTERN PIECES

- ☐ 1x front bodice and 1x front bodice lining (on fold)
- ☐ 2x side back bodice and 2x side back lining
- ☐ 2x straps (4cm wide x 50cm long)
- ☐ 2x ties (9cm wide x 90cm long)
- ☐ 1x elastic channel (4cm wide x about 30cm long)
- ☐ 1x top skirt tier
  - Width = 1.5x waist measurement, for me this is 116cm
  - Length = 34cm
- ☐ 1x middle skirt tier
  - Width = 1.5x width of tier 1, for me this is 174cm
  - Length = 34cm
- ☐ 1x bottom skirt tier
  - Width = 1.5x width of tier 2, for me this is 261cm
  - Length = 34cm

SEWING THE DRESS

PREPARING THE BODICE

1. Stay stitch armholes of bodice and lining
2. Sew darts in bodice and lining
3. Sew bodice pieces right sides together at side seams. Press open. Repeat for lining bodice

SEWING THE STRAPS & TIES

4. Create straps by folding strip in half along long edge, right sides together, and sewing down length. Trim seam allowances and press flat in middle of strap. Turn to right side and press flat again (see "Turning Tubes" on page 48)
5. Create adjustable straps (see page 96)
6. Create ties with a point by folding strip in half along long edge, right sides together, and sewing down length and pointed end. Trim and clip seam allowances and turn to right side. Press flat. See "Build from the Basics" for more details on creating points on the ties

COMPLETING THE BODICE

7. Place your outer bodice right side up. Pin the straps and ties on top of the outer bodice, as per steps 7 and 18 of on pages 86–87. The straps should sit at the outer edges of the front bodice, leaving a 1.5cm gap at the armhole, and 8cm from the centre edge of the back bodice. Make sure they are not twisted. The ties should sit at the top of centre back, leaving a 1.5cm gap at the top edge of the bodice.
8. Baste the straps and ties in place
9. Place the bodice lining on top of this, with the right side of the lining facing the right side of the outer bodice, and pin in place
10. Sew around all bodice edges except the waist seam
11. Trim and clip seam allowances, turn to right side. The straps and ties should now sit nicely at the corners of the bodice
12. Understitch lining where possible – you will not be able to reach into all of the corners
13. Press whole bodice and baste layers at waist seam

SEWING THE SKIRT

14. Hem bottom tier with 1.5cm hem allowance. Gather top edge of bottom tier to fit middle tier
15. Sew middle tier into loop, finish seams and press open
16. Sew bottom tier to middle tier, right sides together, finish seam and press upwards
17. Gather top edge of middle tier
18. Sew top tier into loop, finish seams and press open (add pockets during this step if you are choosing to)
19. Sew middle tier to top tier, right sides together, finish seam and press upwards
20. Gather top edge of top tier but leaving ⅓ of centre back free of gathering stitches as we will not be gathering this section
21. Sew gathered skirt edge to bodice, right sides together, placing the edge of the gathers at the start of the bodice and leaving centre back skirt free between back bodice pieces
22. Finish the full waist seam without cutting any seam allowance off and press upwards to bodice

COMPLETING THE DRESS

23. Measure how long your elastic casing needs to be to cover the exposed skirt edge of the back ⅓ of your skirt plus a few cm at either side. Trim if needed
24. Finish short edges of elastic casing
25. Press long edges of elastic casing in by 1cm and press this in half again to enclose raw edges
26. Pin the elastic casing over the exposed edge of the back skirt, continuing a few centimetres past where the bodice begins at either side
27. Topstitch this in place, about 2mm from edge of elastic casing
28. Insert elastic into this casing using a safety pin. Insert only enough elastic to make the dress tighter on your waist
29. Pin either end of the elastic in place
30. Try the skirt on to check the length of elastic is correct, shorten or lengthen as needed
31. Stitch the elastic down at either end of the elastic casing (only catching the elastic casing and seam allowance underneath, do not sew through the bodice)
32. Trim any excess elastic

CREATING ADJUSTABLE STRAPS

Adjustable straps are a great skill to have in your arsenal. They are most often used on bra straps but can also be used in other items of clothing. I like having adjustable straps on dresses and tops because it can be really tricky to measure the correct length of strap you need for yourself. Using adjustable straps ensures you will get a perfect fit every time and means the garment can adjust to your body as it changes.

STEPS

1. Cut 2 rectangles of fabric each 4cm x 50cm
2. Fold in half lengthways, right sides together, and sew down length of tube with 1cm seam allowance
3. Trim and press seam allowance open
4. Turn tubes to right side and press flat with seam allowance in middle of tube
5. Cut 8cm length off each strap so you are left with 2x 8cm and 2x 42cm
6. With the long lengths, lace one end through slider as seen in picture
7. Sew across strap end to secure
8. Lace remaining end through ring and back through slider as seen in picture
9. With the short lengths, loop through the ring and double back to pin the strap together. Make sure the seam is on the inside of the loop. Stitch loop together 1cm from raw edge
10. You now have a completed strap. Repeat for the other one and continue with project

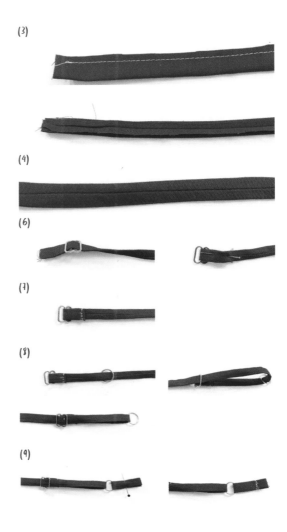

REFASHION
PUFFY SLEEVE CROP TOP

The next step of this pattern alteration process is adding sleeves and learning how to shirr fabric! This technique allows non-stretch fabrics to have stretch and is really easy to do. Adding the shirred back panel to this top ensures it will be wearable for years to come even with body changes and also makes it more comfortable to wear. It is very transferrable and can be used in lots of other projects you do!

I paired the cropped top with puffy sleeves. You will need to source a men's shirt, or of course you could use fabric if you prefer. Choosing a gingham shirt to work from gives my top a more casual summery look that is versatile in my wardrobe. Feel free to choose any colour or pattern you fancy!

Patterns needed: basic bodice and sleeve blocks

Techniques learned: shirring

Seam allowances: 1.5cm unless otherwise stated

NOTION LIST:
- Matching thread
- 1cm wide elastic, up to 1.5m
- Elastic thread

PATTERN PIECES

- ☐ 1x front (on fold)
- ☐ 2x side back
- ☐ 1x centre back
- ☐ 2x sleeve

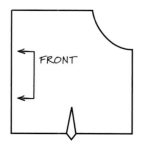
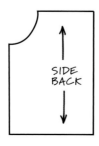

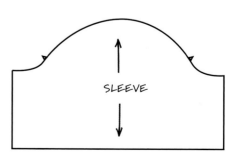

MAKING THE PATTERN

FRONT

1. Measure 5cm towards centre of front bodice, at level of the lowest armhole notch and mark a point A
2. From this point, create a new armhole curve
3. Draw a line perpendicular to centre front to meet point A – this is our new front neckline
4. Add 1.5cm to top of front neckline
5. Remove 10cm of length from bodice to make cropped (you can omit this step if you prefer a waist-length top)

SIDE BACK

1. Measure 5cm towards centre of back bodice, at level of the lowest armhole notch, and mark a point B
2. From this point, create a new armhole curve
3. Draw a line perpendicular to centre front to meet point B – this is our new back neckline
4. Add 1.5cm to top of back neckline
5. Draw a line from top of dart point to meet new back neckline
6. Add 1.5cm seam allowance onto new vertical seam
7. Remove 10cm from bottom edge of bodice

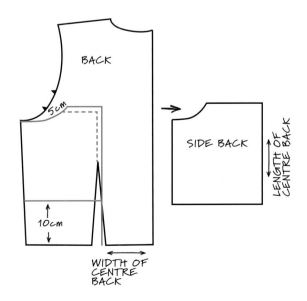

CENTRE BACK

1. Centre back is a rectangle
2. Length = same length as side back centre-most edge
3. Width = centre back to start of back dart x2

SLEEVE

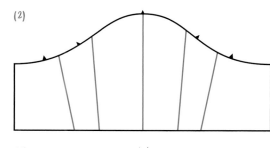

(2)

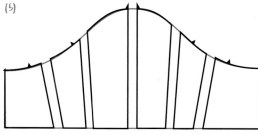

(5)

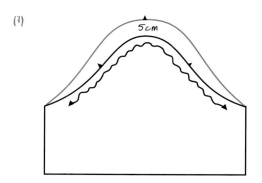

(7)

1. Start with a basic T-shirt length sleeve block
   - Measure 11cm down the side seam from the armhole and draw a line straight across the sleeve pattern to get a T-shirt length block
2. Draw about 5 lines from hem to armhole, spacing them evenly along the pattern piece
3. Make sure these lines only start after the first notch on either side as we do not want to add extra volume that close into the armhole
4. Cut these lines
5. Separate the pattern pieces out evenly, to add 50% to the hem length
   - For example, if your hem started at 50cm long, you want to space out the pattern pieces until the hem is 75cm long, keeping the hemline as straight as possible
6. Draw new lines for the hem and armhole
7. Extend the sleeve by 5cm at the shoulder seam notch and grade this into the armhole edge. Transfer notches

CUTTING OUT

For this top, I cut the front bodice from the front of the shirt, ensuring the buttons sat in the centre front. The side back pieces were cut from the back of the shirt. The shirred section was cut from the sleeves – I had to piece this together.

The sleeve pieces were cut from the lower front and back shirt. For the sleeve cut from the front of the shirt, I first cut out the button placket and stitched the fabric back together. This was so the button placket wasn't in my final sleeve piece as it would have weighed it down.

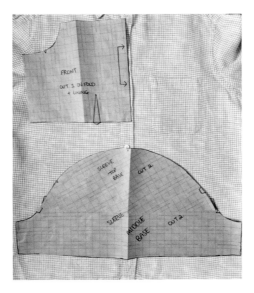

SEWING THE TOP

SEWING THE BODICE

1. Topstitch the button placket closed along the original topstitch lines – you may need to remove the buttons to do this fully, but you can just sew them back on afterwards
2. Sew the darts in the front bodice
3. Sew the front bodice to side back pieces at the side seams, right sides together. Finish seams and press open
4. Hem the bodice at top necklines and bottom edge using 1.5cm allowance
5. Hem the centre back section at the top and bottom by 1.5cm
6. Shirr the centre back section (see page 107)
7. Sew centre back onto side back, right sides together. Finish seam and press towards side back

PREPARING THE SLEEVES

8. Sew sleeve side seams right sides together, finish edges and press open
9. Finish hem edge of sleeve and press up by 1.5cm
10. Pin along the hem, leaving an 8cm opening
11. Stitch around the hem at 1.2cm, leaving this gap unsewn
12. Measure how much elastic you will need for this sleeve hem (mine was 26cm)

13. Insert into the channel using a safety pin. Once you have brought the elastic all the way around, stitch into a loop and push back into hem.
14. Stitch the 8cm gap down with a 1.2cm allowance

SEWING SLEEVES INTO BODICE

15. Pin the sleeve, right sides together, to the armhole. Pin the side seam to sleeve side seam, and pin first sleeve notch to match the front/back edge of the neckline. Pin in between these spots, easing the fabric where needed
16. Stitch along this pinned edge
17. Finish this seam and the rest of the free edge of the sleeve, without taking any seam allowance off
18. Press the seam allowance towards the sleeve
19. For the free edge of the sleeve, press the seam allowance back (1.5cm) and pin in place. You will need to ease/gather the seam allowance into the sleeve in places, especially around the sleeve cap
20. Stitch this at 1.2cm, starting and ending where the stitching is for the top hem of the bodice
21. This stitching has now created a channel into which you can insert your elastic using a safety pin.
22. Pin the elastic at either end of the channel, try the top on to check the length of the elastic is correct
23. Stitch the elastic down at either end, following the stitching line of the top hem of the bodice and backstitching over the elastic a few times to make sure it is secure

(16)

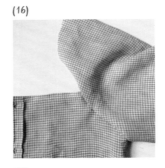

(19)

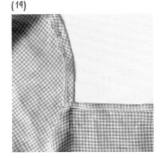

(20)

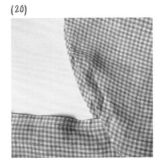

(21)

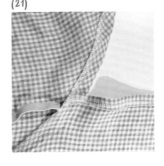

SHIRRING

Shirring is used to turn a non-stretch piece of fabric into a stretchy one. This makes it easier to fit clothes and makes them more comfortable to wear. Plus, it is incredibly easy to do! You will need to buy elastic thread (easily bought in fabric shops or online) and have a spare bobbin and thread to match your project.

1. Hand wind a bobbin with the elastic thread
2. Thread your machine with the top thread to match your fabric and the elastic bobbin
3. Draw parallel lines on your project where you want to sew the lines – I recommend sewing them about 7mm apart and using your sewing machine foot as a guide
4. Stitch each line with a backstitch – making sure not to sew puckers into the fabric
5. Press the fabric using lots of steam – you will notice the piece shrinking as you steam it
6. Continue with the project

THE
RUFFLE DRESS

FRONT

BACK

FIRST THINGS FIRST

She's bright pink, she's got ruffles, she's got a babydoll waist — what else do you need to make a cute girly dress? I paired it with some chunky black boots — a style I love. Keeping the dress quite short and voluminous balances out the big sleeves. Plus, I added some side seam pockets because we all love pockets.

This dress builds on the pattern alterations we made in previous sections of this chapter. Here I have created more complex sleeves that add a fun detail, but you can choose to have regular puffy sleeves if you prefer that style, just follow the pattern alteration and sewing instructions for the sleeves in the previous project.

Patterns needed: bodice block, sleeve block

Techniques learned: elastic channel, crinoline, shirring

Seam allowances: 1.5cm unless otherwise stated

NOTION LIST:
- Matching thread
- 1cm wide elastic, up to 1m
- Elastic thread
- Crinoline (optional), as long as skirt hem and up to 5cm wide
- Rolled hem foot (optional, not technically a notion but something you will need if you want to do a rolled hem)

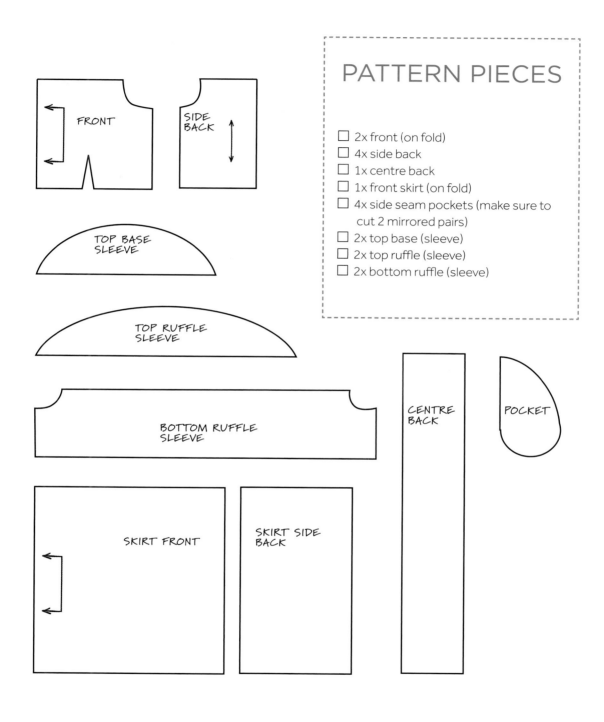

PATTERN PIECES

☐ 2x front (on fold)
☐ 4x side back
☐ 1x centre back
☐ 1x front skirt (on fold)
☐ 4x side seam pockets (make sure to cut 2 mirrored pairs)
☐ 2x top base (sleeve)
☐ 2x top ruffle (sleeve)
☐ 2x bottom ruffle (sleeve)

FRONT

SIDE BACK

TOP BASE SLEEVE

TOP RUFFLE SLEEVE

BOTTOM RUFFLE SLEEVE

CENTRE BACK

POCKET

SKIRT FRONT

SKIRT SIDE BACK

✂ MAKING THE PATTERN

FRONT

1. Measure 5cm towards centre of front bodice, at level of the lowest armhole notch, and mark a point A
2. From this point, create a new armhole curve
3. Draw a line perpendicular to centre front to meet point A – this is our new front neckline
4. Add 1.5cm to top of front neckline
5. Remove 10cm of length from bodice to make cropped (you can omit this step if you prefer a waist-length top)

SIDE BACK

1. Measure 5cm towards centre of back bodice, at level of the lowest armhole notch, and mark a point B
2. From this point, create a new armhole curve
3. Draw a line perpendicular to centre front to meet point B – this is our new back neckline
4. Add 1.5cm to top of back neckline
5. Draw a line from top of dart point to meet new back neckline
6. Add 1.5cm seam allowance onto new vertical seam
7. Remove 10cm from bottom of bodice

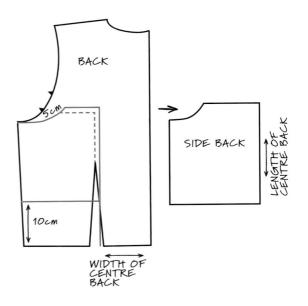

CENTRE BACK

1. Centre back is a rectangle
2. Length = same length as side back pattern centre-most edge plus length of skirt pieces minus 3cm
   - For example, my side back measured 25cm and length of skirt is 63.5cm
   - Total length = 88.5cm - 3cm = 85.5cm
3. Width = centre back to start of back dart x2 of basic bodice block
   - For example, my centre back to start of dart measurement is 9cm, so my total width of centre back is 18cm

SLEEVES

Start with the sleeve created on page 103.

TOP BASE

1. Measure 14.5cm from shoulder notch and draw line straight across
2. Cut across this line
3. Add seam allowance onto bottom of this piece
4. Draw about 5 lines from hem to armhole, spacing them evenly along the pattern piece
5. Make sure these lines only start after the first notch on either side as we do not want to add extra volume that close into the armhole. Cut these lines
6. Separate the pattern pieces out evenly, to add 50% to the hem length
   - For example, if your hem started at

FRONT SKIRT

1. Width should be about 2x width of front bodice
2. Length should be however long you want to make it
3. Mine is 1m wide x 63.5cm long

SIDE BACK SKIRT

1. Width should be about 2x width of side back bodice
2. Length should be however long you want to make it
3. Mine is 36cm wide x 63.5cm long

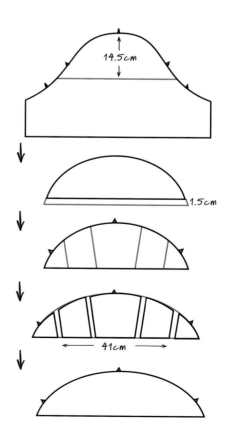

50cm long, you want to space out the pattern pieces until the hem is 75cm long, keeping the hemline as straight as possible

7. Draw new lines for the hem and armhole

TOP RUFFLE

1. Take top base piece you have just created
2. Draw about 5 lines from hem to armhole, spacing them evenly along the pattern piece
3. Make sure these lines only start after the first notch on either side as we do not want to add extra volume that close into the armhole
4. Cut these lines
5. Separate the pattern pieces out evenly, to add 50% to the hem length
   - For example, if your hem started at 50cm long, you want to space out the pattern pieces until the hem is 75cm long, keeping the hemline as straight as possible
6. Add 3cm to length of hem
7. Draw new lines for the hem and armhole

BOTTOM RUFFLE

1. Take bottom section you drew back when you were making the top base
2. Add 1.5cm seam allowance to top of this section
3. Cut bottom section in half and extend to make hem about 50% longer
4. Add length to your desire, I made my bottom ruffle 16cm long

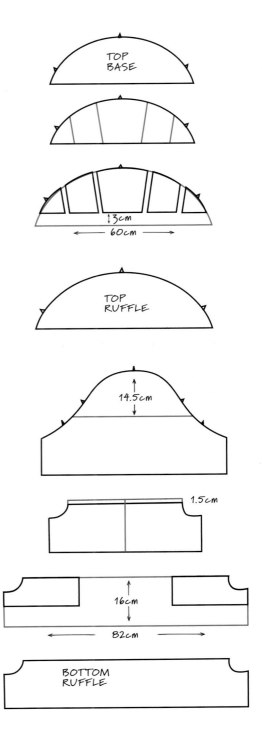

SEWING THE DRESS

We will be making two separate bodices. One as the outer bodice, and one as the lining bodice.

PREPARING THE BODICE

1. Sew darts into bodice and lining
2. Sew side seams of bodice and lining bodice, by sewing right sides together and pressing open
3. Pin and sew straight neck edges of lining and bodice right sides together for front and back, trim seam allowance, turn bodice right sides out and understitch these seams, press
4. Baste all other sides of bodice at 1cm – armholes, centre back and waist edges
5. Hem top edge of centre back piece by 1.5cm
6. Shirr the centre back section (see instructions on page 107) making the shirring end at the waistline of your dress

SEWING THE SKIRT

7. Finish curved pocket edges
8. Sew the straight edge of the pocket to the side seam of the skirt, right sides together, placing the top of the pocket 11cm from the top of the skirt waist edge
9. Finish side seam edges
10. Stitch side seams, from edge of waist to top notch of pockets, rotate dress to sew around curved edge until you meet the side seam again, add back stitches. Restart stitching side seam where bottom pocket notch is and carry on until hem
11. Clip back dress seam allowance under pocket to allow you to press seam open below level of the pocket
12. Press pocket and seam allowance above pocket to front of dress
13. Gather top edge of skirt

CONSTRUCTING THE DRESS

14. Sew skirt onto side back and front bodice, finish seam and press up
15. Sew centre back section to rest of dress, right sides together, matching up top edge of bodice and end of shirring to the waist seam
16. Finish and press seams

SEWING THE SLEEVES

17. Hem edges of sleeve ruffles with 1cm hem allowance – I used a rolled hem foot
18. Gather and sew the bottom ruffle onto the top base right sides together, finish and press seam away from gathers
19. Gather the curved edge of the top ruffle and pin onto the curved edge of the top base. Baste this in place
20. Now treat the sleeves as one piece and complete "Sewing the Sleeves" section of the previous project

FINISHING TOUCHES

21. Hem skirt using double turned edge or crinoline to make it stand out

CRINOLINE

(1)

(2)

(3)

(4)

(5)

Crinoline is a stiff strip of plastic that you can sew into hems to create volume in garments. I first used it during my time on *The Great British Sewing Bee*, but before that had thought it was a tricky skill. I was very, very wrong; it is very, very easy. Not only easy, but it is cheap to buy and gives your projects impact. Here are 8 simple steps for using crinoline.

1. Finish the edge of your hem
2. Pin crinoline to the right side of the fabric, lining it up with the edge of the fabric. When you have pinned around the whole hem, overlap the crinoline by a few centimetres
3. Sew around hem at 7mm
4. Press the crinoline upwards (gently, use very low heat and don't hold down for long at all)
5. Roll the crinoline inside the hem so there is a small 7mm strip of fabric on the inside of the hem
6. Press this flat and pin top of crinoline around hem
7. Sew to secure crinoline down, about 7mm away from free edge of crinoline
8. Press

CHAPTER 7

TIE BACK
PATTERN ALTERATION

Backless dresses have been a love of mine for as long as I can remember, and I knew I had to design one for my book.

The exact design of this bodice was actually inspired by a woman I met in the John Lewis toilets in Liverpool. She was wearing sage green high-waisted trousers, which I told her I loved, and a white puffy sleeve top with an open back, which I loved in secret as I didn't want to seem creepy. I can't remember the exact design of her top, so I took some artistic licence. Thank you, random woman, for you inspiration. It does seem to strike at the most unexpected moments.

When I showed my dad the finished top for this chapter, he said, "It looks really cool . . . but you don't wear a bra with it?" . . . No dad, I don't. Bubble burst. This design naturally will show any bra you wear, so, the options are:

- No bra
- Sew bra cups into the bodice lining (for the dress project)
- Wear a bra with fancy back to show it off
- Wear any bra or undergarment and don't care what people say

Your choice!

MAKING THE PATTERN

Patterns needed: bodice and sleeve block

Front bodice remains the same as basic block

BACK BODICE

1. Mark 10cm down the side seam from underarm = A
2. Mark 2cm up from this = B
3. Mark 2cm in from centre back neck = C
4. Make line from A to C, make it slightly curved towards side seam
5. Add 1.5cm seam allowance along this curved edge

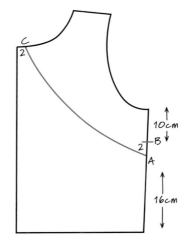

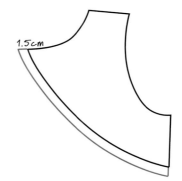

TIES WITH ANGLED OFF ENDS

(See "Build from the Basics" (page 49) to learn how to add points.)

1. Width = (B to waist seam) x 2 = 32cm for me
2. Length = 110cm total

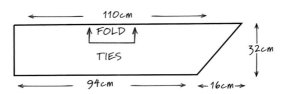

SLEEVES

1. Start with a basic sleeve block. You can choose to make the sleeves any length
    *   I chose a T-shirt length sleeve for the top and ¾ length sleeve for the dress
    *   T-shirt length: measure 11cm down the side seam from the armhole and draw a line straight across the sleeve pattern
    *   ¾ length: measure 35cm down the side seam from the armhole and draw a line straight across the sleeve pattern
2. Draw about 5 lines from hem to armhole, spacing them evenly along the pattern piece
3. Make sure these lines only start after the first notch on either side – we do not want to add extra volume that close into the armhole
4. Cut these lines
5. Separate the pattern pieces out evenly, to add 50% to the hem length
    *   For example, if your hem started at 50cm long, you want to space out the pattern pieces until the hem is 75cm long, keeping the hemline as straight as possible
6. Draw new lines for the hem and armhole
7. You will only be gathering between notches

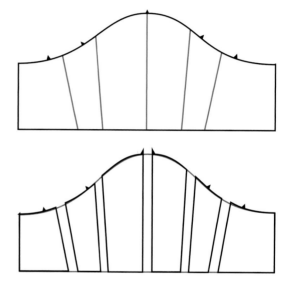

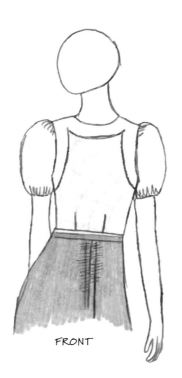

FRONT

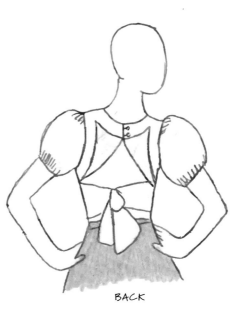

BACK

REFASHION
BACKLESS CROP TOP

The top version of this pattern can be made from something second-hand – I chose this white shift dress. I was drawn to it because of the sheer overlayer which I knew would make a cute sleeve feature. For the bodice, I kept the underneath fabric for coverage, but treated the pieces as one. Therefore, the steps in this project do not result in a lined bodice. I simply removed the original dress lining from the sleeves.

Techniques learned: bias binding

Seam allowances: 1.5cm unless otherwise stated

NOTION LIST:
- Matching thread
- Bias binding – or make your own, see "Build from the Basics" (page 40)

DRESS REQUIREMENTS:
- Shift dress in your size (at least low-thigh length)
- Shoulders of dress sit on or near your shoulders (no further than a few cm away)
- Dress neckline you like – if altering, follow instructions in next project (page 138)
- The dress should have a closure at the back neckline – most likely a button
- Lighter weight fabrics are ideal for this project, as they allow the sleeves to be puffy but not heavy!

PATTERN PIECES

- ☐ 1x front bodice (on fold)
- ☐ 2x back bodice
- ☐ 2x sleeves
- ☐ 2x ties
- ☐ 1x bias binding

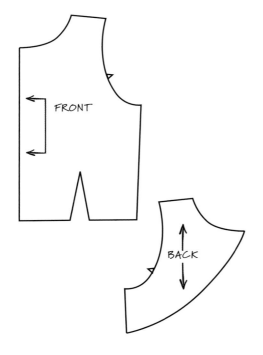

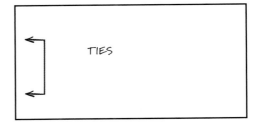

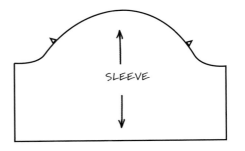

CUTTING OUT

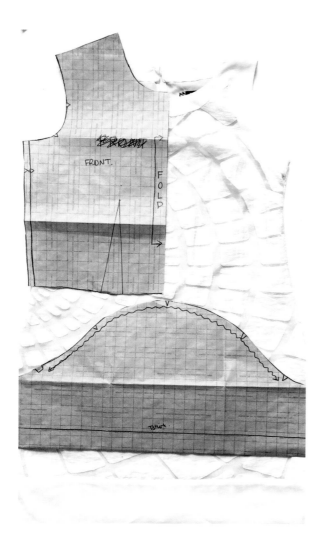

The bodice of this top will be made from the bodice of the original dress you have. Place your front bodice block onto the dress and cut across the bottom. This is what we will be starting with when sewing our bodice.

Cut the sleeves from lower portion of the dress. The armhole of the dress is not going to perfectly match the armhole of your bodice block. However, we are making puffy sleeves which have gathers around the armhole, making them much more forgiving and allowing for a slightly different armhole shape. If you are buying a dress in your size, the armholes should be very similar to those of your bodice block anyway.

The ties will be made from the very bottom of the dress. Make them as long as you can from the fabric you have. Mine ended up being shorter than the ideal length but the top was still able to be tied, so it was fine.

SEWING THE TOP

PREPARING THE BODICE

1. Sew darts into front bodice and lining
2. Unpick side seams until about 5cm away from armhole.
3. Open out the top so the back bodice lies flat. Pin both sides together to keep in place. Trace and then cut back bodice piece.

When cutting, I altered the centre back slightly, so it ended 1cm down from the white band on my dress neckline. This was so I didn't have to bias bind many layers of fabric. You can decide if you need to alter the back bodice curve slightly to fit into your dress. You should make the final back bodice edge finish around 1cm from your back closure. Therefore, the cut you make should be 1cm away from this.

4. Unpin back bodice and lay flat. (See photo)
5. If you need to, stitch along edge to secure two layers of fabric

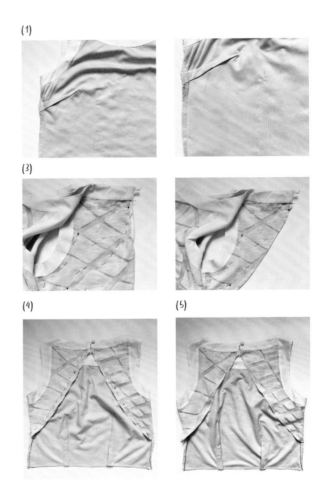

Top Tip

When sewing darts through two layers of fabric, first draw the dart outline in chalk, including the middle line. Sew this middle line through both layers until a few mm away from the dart point. This helps keep the two layers together, so you don't end up with a bubble at the top of your dart. Sew dart as normal and press towards centre front.

6. Finish the back bodice edge with bias binding (see page 40), so it is not visible. I made mine from spare lining fabric. You can either make some or use ready-made. To enclose the raw edges of the bias binding at the centre back edge, fold in the short edge of the bias binding by 1cm before you carry out the last step of the binding process

7. Finish the bottom edge of front bodice. If your edge is straight, you can hem it; if it is curved, you can use bias binding. Use a 1.5cm allowance

8. Make ties. For each tie, fold along long edge with fabric right sides together and created pointed end if you have enough fabric and if you have not done so already. Mine did not have pointed ends as my dress didn't have quite enough fabric

9. Pin along short end and complete length of long edge

10. Sew along these edges

11. Trim and clip seam allowances

12. Turn the tube to the right side, through the free short end. Press the ties flat

13. Place the bodice inside out

14. Pin the ties onto the front bodice right sides together, matching bottom edges

15. Pin free edge of back bodice on top of these layers

16. Stitch the side seams. Finish edges and press to front

(6)

(7)

(13)

(16)

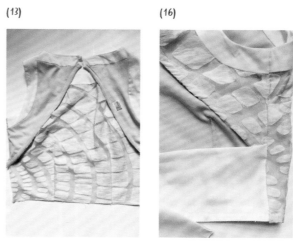

PREPARING SLEEVES

1. Sew side seam of sleeves, right sides together
2. Finish the raw edges and press seam open
3. Finish bottom edge of sleeve
4. Press sleeve hem up by 1.5cm. Pin around edge, leaving a gap of about 6cm
5. Sew around hem at 1.2cm, leaving the 6cm open
6. Measure the length of elastic you need
7. Insert this elastic into the sleeve hem using a safety pin
8. Sew the elastic into a loop with plenty of backstitching
9. Insert elastic back into channel and sew 6cm gap closed at 1.2cm keeping elastic out of the way
10. Finish armhole edge of sleeves
11. Gather armhole edge of sleeve between notches

CONSTRUCTING THE TOP

1. Pin sleeve into armhole by inserting sleeve 1.5cm under finished edge of bodice armhole. Right side of sleeve should be touching wrong side of armhole. Follow notches and make gathers even around armhole
2. Topstitch sleeve in, 2mm away from edge of finished bodice edge. You can do another row 1cm away from this edge too to secure seam allowance if you want
3. Remove gathering stitches from sleeve
4. Press seam

(1)

FINISHING THE NECK

If your dress already has a wider feature at the top of the back neck, like mine does, then you can add an extra button and loop to secure the top a bit more.

If you chose to alter your dress neckline, or are using fabric, follow instructions for completing the neckline in the next project.

THE
ROMANTIC DRESS

FIRST THINGS FIRST

The dress version of this pattern is perfect for summer. The short skirt complements the slightly longer sleeves, which can be worn bunched up for extra volume. Feel free to add tiers or gathers to this skirt to make the design your own!

When picking fabric, you could choose one that has good drape, so you get a nice soft skirt, such as viscose, or one with a bit more hold, such as a cotton lawn/poplin. I chose the latter because I loved the colour and wanted more structured sleeves. If you choose a drapey fabric, you should interface the tie pieces to help them stand out and beware that your sleeves won't stand up!

This is not the first version of this dress I created. You can read about my design process for this skirt in "A Note on Designing" after the instructions (page 141).

Techniques learned: bias binding, gathering, zip

Seam allowances: 1.5cm unless otherwise stated

NOTION LIST:
- Matching thread
- 1cm wide elastic, up to 1.5m
- Bias binding – make your own, see "Build from the Basics" (page 40)
- 20–25.5cm zip in matching colour

PATTERN PIECES

- ☐ 1x front bodice piece (on fold)
- ☐ 1x front bodice lining (on fold)
- ☐ 2x sleeves
- ☐ 2x back bodice piece
- ☐ 2x back bodice lining
- ☐ 2x ties
- ☐ 1x front A-line skirt (on fold)
- ☐ 1x back A-line skirt (on fold)

TIES

BIAS BINDING FOR NECKLINE

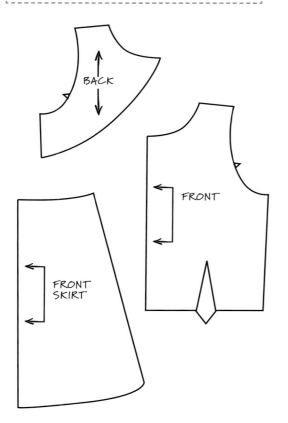

BACK

FRONT

FRONT SKIRT

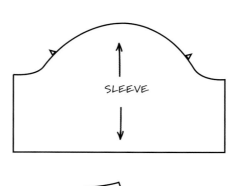

SLEEVE

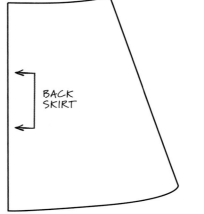

BACK SKIRT

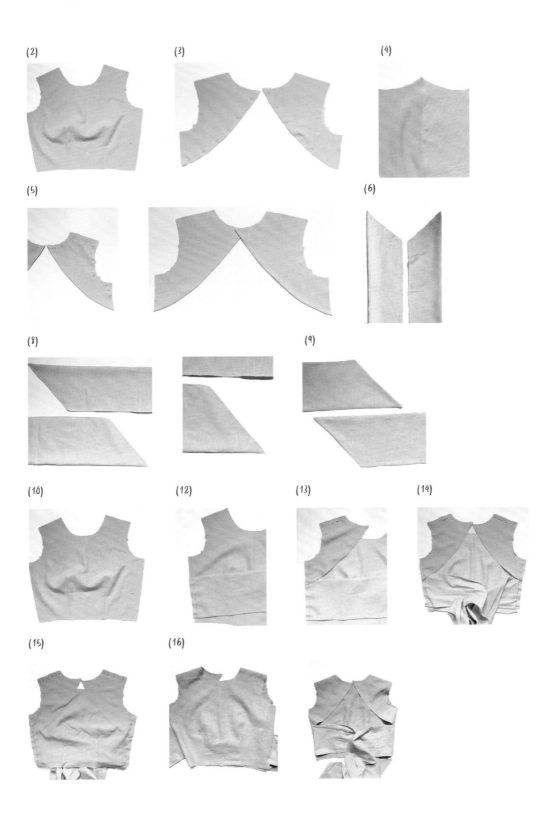

(2)

(3)

(4)

(5)

(6)

(8)

(9)

(10)

(12)

(13)

(14)

(15)

(16)

MAKING THE PATTERN

Besides the pattern alterations on page 120, an A-line skirt is the only new pattern we need to use for the dress. We will be using the A-line skirt block. Make any size adjustments necessary and then cut the pattern to the length of skirt you want. My skirt was 53cm long, giving me a shorter dress. Remember to include a hem allowance here!

SEWING THE DRESS

PREPARING THE BODICE

1. Stay stich front and back bodice neckline
2. Sew darts into front bodice (and lining)
3. Place back lining bodice pieces on back bodice pieces, right sides together. Sew only the curved free edge of these pieces. Trim seam allowance and turn to right side
4. Understitch these seams
5. Press flat. Baste all other edges of back bodice
6. Make ties. For each tie, fold along long edge and created pointed end if you have not done so already
7. Pin along diagonal line and complete length of long edge
8. Trim and clip seam allowances
9. Turn the tube to the right side, through the free short end. You can use a pin or point turner (a sewing tool) to make the point pointy! Press the ties flat

10. Place the front bodice right side up
12. Pin the ties onto the front bodice. Leave 1.5cm at the bottom of the side seam and place the seam of the ties closest to the waist of the bodice
13. Pin the back bodice pieces on, right sides together
14. You can baste these seams down at this point if you want to
15. Place the front lining onto the front bodice, right sides facing and pin at shoulder and side seams
16. Sew these seams. Trim them and turn bodice right sides out. All the raw edges of the shoulder and side seams will be enclosed. Press the seams flat
17. Baste remaining bodice and lining edges together – around front neckline, armhole and waistline

SEWING THE SLEEVES

1. Sew side seam of sleeves, right sides together
2. Finish the raw edges and press seam open
3. Finish bottom edge of sleeve
4. Press sleeve hem up by 1.5cm. Pin around edge, leaving a gap of about 6cm
5. Sew around hem at 1.2cm, leaving the 6cm open
6. Measure the length of elastic you need
7. Insert this into the sleeve hem using a safety pin
8. Sew the elastic into a loop with plenty of backstitching
9. Insert elastic back into channel and sew 6cm gap closed at 1.2cm keeping elastic out of the way
10. Gather armhole edge of sleeve between notches
11. Pin sleeve into armhole right sides together, following notches and making gathers even around armhole
12. Sew armhole seam
13. Remove gathering stitches from sleeve
14. Finish armhole seam and press towards sleeve

COMPLETING THE NECKLINE

15. Prepare your bias binding
16. Sew onto the dress neckline with technique to hide binding, making sure to leave a trail of about 20cm at either side of the back neckline edge. This ensures you can tie the back neck together. See "Build from the Basics" (page 40) to learn how to sew on bias binding.
17. When stitching the binding down in the final step, you should close off the 20cm free edges with a topstitch close to the loose edges, but on the dress neck edge, stitch at 8mm as you normally would to finish bias binding

(1)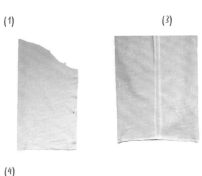

(3)

(4)

(7)

(8)

(9)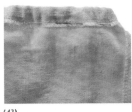

(11)

ADDING THE SKIRT

1. Finish waist and side seam edges of back skirt
2. Finish side seam edges of front skirt
3. On one side seam (the side you want the zip on), pin the side seam with fabric right sides together
4. Place horizontal pins 1.5cm from waist edge and where the zip teeth of the zip will end
5. Stitch from bottom hem up to first horizontal pin (bottom of zip) and do a backstitch
6. Keep the needle down, change the machine settings to the longest stitch length
7. Continue sewing until the next pin and do not do another backstitch
8. Press seam open
9. On the inside, pin the zip to the seam, placing the top of the zip 1.5cm from top edge and make sure the zip teeth match up with the middle of the seam
10. Turn skirt to the right side and pin the zip in place from the right side
11. Remove pins from inside
12. Using a zip foot, sew down one side of the zip, close to the zip teeth (a few mm away from middle of seam)
13. When you get to the bottom (where basting stitches end), put needle in down position and rotate skirt so you can carefully sew across the zip tape and repeat this process so you can sew up the other side of the zip
14. Use a stitch picker to remove the basting stitches you sewed in step 7
    - When doing this, it might help to first keep the zip closed, and start and end sewing 3cm away from waist edge. Then unzip the zip to get the zip tie out of the way and go back to sew the top 3cm of zip into place on either side
15. Press zip
16. Sew the other side seam with right sides together and press seam open

(3)

(4)

(7)

(9)

(11)

(13)

SEWING THE SKIRT TO THE BODICE

(1)

1. Fold waist edge of back skirt inwards by 1.5cm along whole length and pin into place
2. Stitch along this edge at 1.2cm
3. Insert elastic using a safety pin, pin the elastic at either end before cutting it so you can try the skirt on and make sure it is the right length. At this point, your skirt should fit comfortably around your waist. Once it is comfortable you can stitch the elastic in place at either end of the back waist and trim off any excess

(3)

4. Pin the front skirt onto your front bodice, with right sides together
5. Stitch this seam
6. Finish seam and press upwards. Using a few hand stitches, tack the seam allowance onto the bodice lining to keep it in place
7. Try dress on and make sure the length is what you want (remember there is a hem allowance)
8. Hem skirt using hem allowance you included

A NOTE ON DESIGNING

The design of this dress took multiple forms. I was set on the bodice design from the start, but the skirt was a bit less obvious. Since the back of the bodice is so open, I wanted to make sure the front was more closed, for balance.

The first version of this dress I designed was full length, with a long top-skirt tier and short ruffle on the bottom. I spent ages making it, and it was completed. I tried it on and hated it. I looked, and this is honestly the only way I can explain it, like a wench. I think it was mostly to do with my choice of fabric (linen) and length of skirt tiers; they ended up looking a bit off. I desperately tried to fix it by adding a slit, but it just wasn't right. I had picked a heavy-ish linen fabric and I knew I needed to change it.

So, I started again, chose a lightweight cotton lawn, and also decided to make an A-line skirt over a gathered one. The change to skirt pattern balanced the design and was more flattering. This fabric and simple skirt change truly trans-formed how the garment looked and how I felt wearing it. Making the dress again also gave me a chance to fine-tune the bodice design. Refashioning your own makes is just like refashioning second-hand clothes. And I need to find a plan for refashioning the first linen version of my yellow dress.

I guess the point of the story is, designing clothes is an evolving process. Please don't be disheartened if you spend hours making something, try it on and instantly get a bad feeling because you don't like it. This happens all the time in sewing, and it still happens to me. There is no point at which we become perfect sewists, we just keep learning. And there are always ways that we can adjust and change garments once they are completed. Also — make sure you pick the right fabric before you start sewing!

Honestly, changing a garment's design is where some of my best makes have come from, including the dress I wore to the NTAs (page 161). This dress was completed (image on page 143) after about 15 hours of work. I tried it on, and it just didn't feel right at all. I re-worked it and ended up with one of my best ever garments. I have an Instagram highlight with a bit more info on this process if you want to know more: find it at @serenasews_.

Accept failure as a part of sewing, mope for 20 minutes, move on and get creative!

FIRST DESIGN

FIRST DESIGN

CHAPTER 8
SKIRTS

SIDE SLIT SKIRT

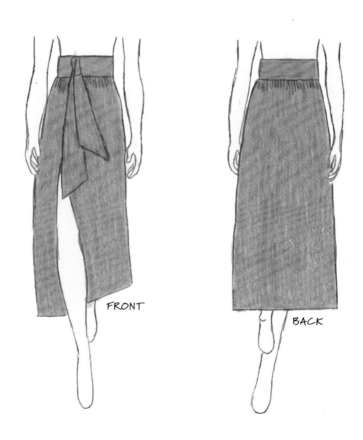

FRONT

BACK

#SERENASEWSSLITSKIRT

FIRST THINGS FIRST

This gathered skirt is a superb beginner skirt project. It can be adjusted so easily to fit your body and style preferences and is very versatile in your wardrobe. I like adding a slit into the front of the skirt for extra flare and ease of movement. The belt is also an additional style feature that adds interest, but the skirt looks great without it too. This will quickly become a summer wardrobe staple for you, so I recommend picking a colour that will go with many other items in your wardrobe, so you always have something to pair it with!

Your fabric should be non-stretch of light to mid-weight, depending what vibe you want the skirt to be. Choose a lighter fabric for a floatier skirt; for example, cotton lawn. I chose to make my red one out of mid-weight cotton, so the finished style is more structured.

Patterns needed: none

Techniques learned: elastic channel, bagging out the belt, waist seam pockets

Seam allowances: 1.5cm unless otherwise stated

NOTION LIST:
- Matching thread
- 2.5cm wide elastic, long enough to fit round your waist

MAKING THE PATTERN

BACK SKIRT

LENGTH

- Decide finished length of skirt, mine is 81cm
- Add hem allowance – mine was 2.5cm
- Add elastic channel allowance at top – 3.5cm
- Add these three measurements to get total length to cut = 87cm

WIDTH

- The width of your final skirt (un-gathered) should be 1.5–2x your waist measurements. How voluminous you make it partly depends on your style preference and fabric type – this red fabric is fairly thick for a cotton and anything more than 1.5x width looked silly.
- My width of final skirt = 112cm (width of final skirt/2) + 3cm
- 112/2 + 3cm
- 66 + 3 = 69cm

FINISHED BACK SKIRT MEASUREMENTS
87cm x 69cm

BELT

- Width = 26cm
- Length = 172cm

I also angled off the ends of mine to make them pointy – see "Build from the Basics" (page 29) to learn how

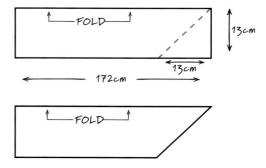

FRONT SKIRT

LENGTH
- Decide length (mine is 81cm).

WIDTH
- Width of final skirt/2 = 66cm
- Decide which side you want slit on
- If you don't want a slit, cut 2x back skirt and skip step 1
- Measure ⅔ along width of skirt and draw line down rectangle
- Cut along this line to create a L and R front skirt – I added my slit onto the right side of the skirt (smaller front section will be side of slit)
- Mark notch for length of slit, mine is 34.5cm from unsewn waist
- Add 1.5cm onto both sides of new slit seam

FINISHED FRONT SKIRT MEASUREMENTS
Right side: 87cm x 23cm
Left side: 87cm x 46cm

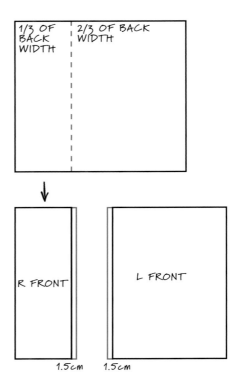

SOME SUGGESTIONS FOR WAYS TO ALTER THE SKIRT EVEN MORE
- Change up the width or length of the belt
- Remove the slit for a closed skirt
- Add a gathered ruffle onto the skirt for a tiered effect

PATTERN PIECES

- ☐ 1x skirt back
- ☐ 1x skirt left front
- ☐ 1x skirt right front
- ☐ 4x waist seam pockets – remember to cut 2 mirrored pairs
- ☐ 1x belt (might have to piece rectangles together to get full width)

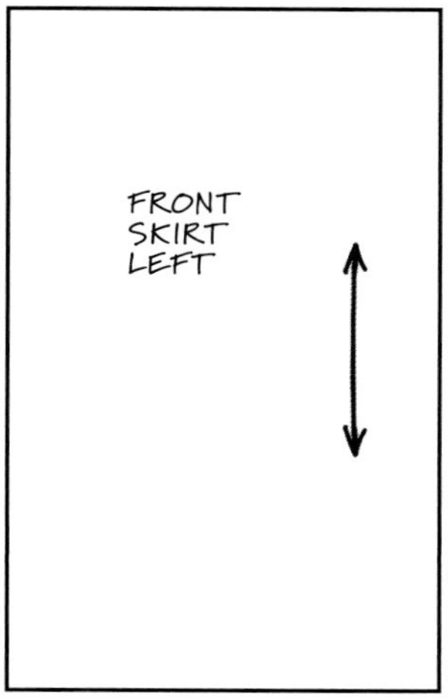

FRONT
SKIRT
LEFT

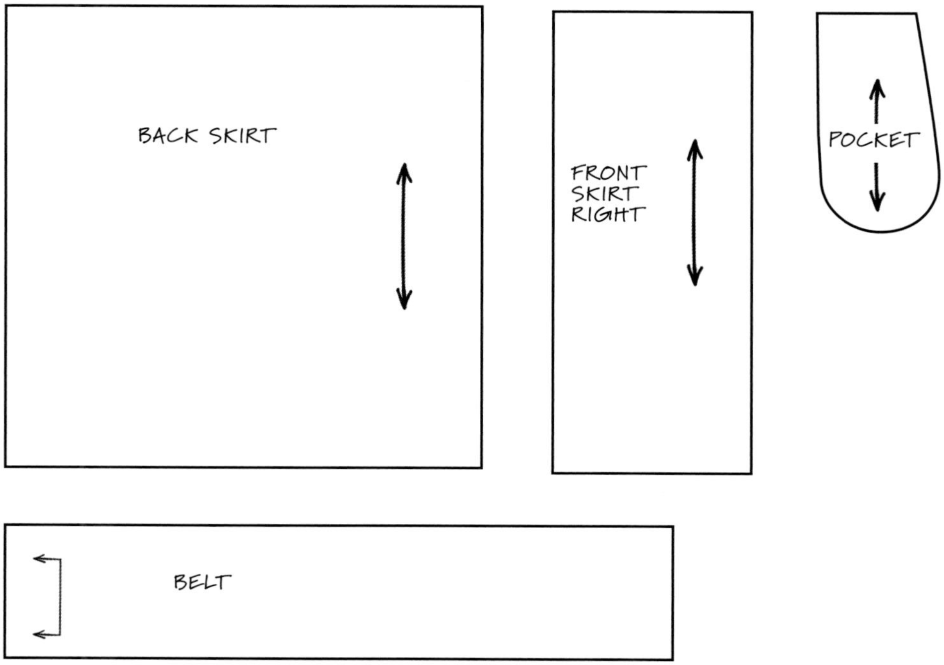

BACK SKIRT

FRONT
SKIRT
RIGHT

POCKET

BELT

SEWING THE SKIRT

1. Make front skirt by finishing edges of slit and stitching the slit from waist down to notch. Press the seam open and press open edges of slit back by 1.5cm. Stitch at 1.2cm, sewing from bottom hem upwards, across start of slit and back down to the hem; creating a rectangle at top of slit
2. Prepare pockets by finishing curved edges
3. Pin pockets to side seams, right sides together, with top of pocket placed 2.5cm away from top edge of skirt
4. Stitch pocket onto side seam of front and back skirt with 1cm seam allowance
5. Finish side seam edges of skirt and press seam towards pocket. Under-stitch this seam
6. Sew side seams, for pockets – sew side seam until first pocket notch, restart stitching side seam where bottom pocket notch is and carry on until hem. Stitch around pocket curve
7. Clip seam allowance under pocket to allow you to press seam open below level of the pocket
8. Press pocket to front and pin top edge in place, it should sit evenly 2.5cm away from top edge of fabric
9. Finish top edge of skirt and press in by 3.5cm
10. Stitch around waist 3cm from edge of fabric, making sure you catch the pocket in the seam – sew from the inside so you can ensure you are catching the pocket. Leave an 8cm opening on back of skirt
11. Measure how much elastic you need to fit your waist and add 2.5cm to account for overlap. The length you need is dependent on how stretchy the elastic is
12. Insert elastic into channel and move around channel using safety pin until it comes out the other side
13. Ensure it is not twisted and overlap edges by 2.5cm then stitch together using a square with cross design and lots of back stitches. Insert elastic back into channel
14. Pin the 8cm opening closed and stitch down
15. Check skirt is length you want, hem according to your allowance
16. Make belt by pinning both pieces right sides together, sew all around with 1cm seam allowance but leave an 8cm opening in the middle of the belt. Add points if you want to (see "Build from the Basics" page 49)
17. Clip and trim all seam allowances
18. Turn belt right side out
19. Press all over including the opening
20. Either hand stitch opening closed or topstitch all around belt edge around 2mm from edge

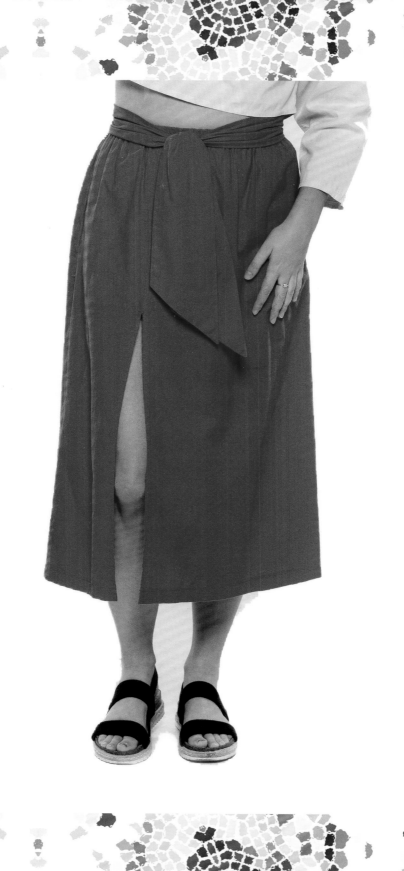

RUCHED SKIRT

FIRST THINGS FIRST

This refashioning project turns a simple maxi dress into a skirt with a sexy slit and ruched detail.

For the project, you will need to source a maxi dress that has a pencil style skirt with at least 3cm of ease around the hips and waist. The dress should NOT be stretchy. I picked this one because I loved the bright orange colour! I was working from a sleeveless dress, so if you find one with sleeves you should have more than enough fabric to work with.

Ideally the dress you find shouldn't have any slit, as we will be adding our own. However, if you find your dream dress and it happens to have a slit, don't worry because you have a couple of options:

1. If the slit is on the same seam as the zip you need to close it: overlap the slit by about 2mm and stitch down the overlap to seal the slit and create a closed pencil skirt (it's what I had to do, and it worked out fine). Continue with the project as normal
2. If the slit is on a different seam to the zip and you don't like the placement of it: overlap the slit by about 2mm and stitch down the overlap to seal the slit and create a closed pencil skirt. Continue with the project as normal
3. If the slit is on a different seam to the zip and you like the placement of it, create the ruching effect straight onto the slit, saving you the effort of making your own

---

Patterns needed: none
Techniques learned: ruching
Seam allowances: 1.5cm unless otherwise stated

NOTION LIST:
- Matching thread
- Hook and eye

SEWING THE SKIRT

(1)

(6)

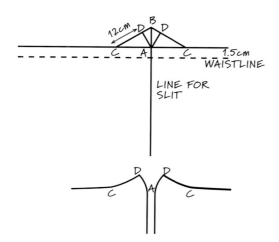

1. Try on the dress and pin where your waistline is. Using a fabric pen, draw a line 1.5cm above this to create seam allowance. This line is where we will be drawing from
2. Mark a line ⅔ of the way along the front of the dress, on the side you want the slit to be (mark A). Make another mark 5cm (see note) above this (mark B) – this will help us create the ruching effect
3. Measure 12cm (see note) either side of mark A and make two more marks (C). Remember this A–C measurement
4. Join B to C at either side of the slit, making the line slightly curved to make the join smooth
5. Take the A–C measurement and measure from C towards mark B at either side, mark two new points (D). A–C for me is 12cm, so I measured 12cm from C towards B
6. Join both D points to point A, again making the lines curve so they join smoothly

Note: if you have a long torso, I recommend lengthening the A–B measurement and vice versa, shortening for a short torso.

The A–C measurement should be approximately one sixth of your total waist measurement. For example: my waist measurement is 73cm, divided by 6 this gives me an A–C measurement of 12.16. I rounded this to an even 12cm.

7. Cut the dress around the new waistline. When doing this, make sure your zip pull is below where you are cutting and ensure you do not pull the zip up without securing the ends of the zip tape. Once cut, secure ends of zip tape with some hand stitches to ensure you do not zip the tie off

8. Cut up slit

9. Baste around all of these edges if your dress has a lining

10. Pin the slit closed to try on your skirt for fitting. I had to remove some fabric from the waist of my skirt to make it fit me properly – I took this in from the darts and the slit seam

11. Pin the slit again and mark down from waistline where you want your slit to end. Remember, this section will be slightly ruched so try to emulate this when pinning and holding. My mark was 48 cm from waistline

12. Finish edges of slit. Sew from waistline down to mark for slit opening and press seam open, and below stitching, press seam allowance back by 1.5cm

13. Cut into the seam allowance just above the slit opening. This allows you to double fold the seam allowance below this to hide the edge of the fabric. Press and pin these hems

14. Sew close to the folded edge, stitching a few cm above the slit opening (to where you cut the

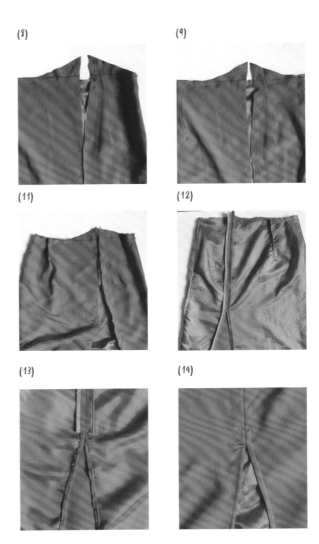

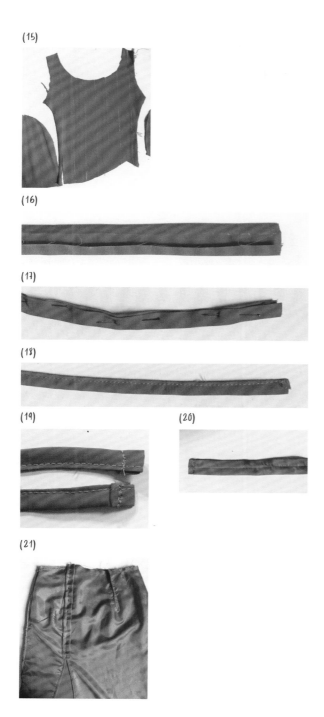

(15)

(16)

(17)

(18)

(19)

(20)

(21)

seam allowance) and pivoting to sew across and down the other side

15. Cut strips for ties – does not need to be on the bias. Mine were 3cm wide and I cut these from remaining scrap of front bodice

16. Create ties by sewing small strips into 2x long strips 85cm long. Fold both long edges into the middle and press

17. Fold this one more time along long edge to hide all raw edges

18. Stitch close to folded edge

19. Fold one end of each tie back by 1cm and then 1cm again to enclose raw edges. Stitch close to folded edge to finish the end of both ties

20. Make channel. I used lining fabric. Cut a piece of fabric 8cm x (length from top of waist to slit + 1cm). Fold in half right sides together along long edge and sew using 1cm seam allowance. Turn right way out and press so seam allowance is in middle. Fold one short edge back by 1cm towards side with the seam and sew in place close to folded edge

21. Sew channel onto slit: place channel onto the inside of the skirt, seam of the channel towards the skirt. Align the middle of the channel with the seam of the slit. Make the short folded edge of the channel sit where the slit opening begins. Pin along the middle of the

channel, trying to match it up with the seam line

22. Turn the skirt to the right side. Now pin along the seam from the right side. You will be sewing the channel down from the right side (for this line of stitching at least). Baste the channel into place and ensure pins have maintained the matching of the seam and middle of the channel. Stitch along the seam line from the top of the waist down to the slit opening from the right side so you can ensure the stitches are in the seam

23. Turn skirt to wrong side. Now stitch two parallel lines at either side of the seam you just sewed – 1cm away from the middle stitch line. This forms our two channels for the ties

24. Remove basting stitches

25. Using a safety pin, insert ties into channels from slit opening and stitch to secure at waist

26. Make bias binding from leftover fabric – see "Build from Basics" (page 29) to learn how

27. Stitch onto waist with method that leaves it visible – this is more suitable as the zip will not fold over into the inside so we cannot do the option of hidden binding

(22)

(23)

(25)

(28)

(29)

(30)

(31)

28. To finish off the edges nicely where the zip is: sew the first binding seam, leaving about 2cm of overhang at either edge.

29. Fold the whole binding up and then fold in half back down, so the right sides of the binding are touching.

30. Sew a line just where the zip ends. Cut off any excess seam allowance to leave only 1cm.

31. Fold this into the inside of the binding, and you should be able to fold the whole way around the waist to conceal the raw edge.

32. Stitch close to the binding folded edge

33. Remove any basting stitches from project

34. Sew a hook and eye on the inside of the binding above the zip to finish

CHAPTER 9

THE
VILLANELLE DRESS

FIRST THINGS FIRST

I designed this dress to wear to the National Television Awards in September 2021. This was a very special event and I was not expecting to be invited. When I heard I was, I had about a month to design a dress fit for the red carpet. A month seems like loads of time – but not when you're doing a full-time medical degree and you have to actually sew the garment yourself! The final dress is so worth the hours and hours I spent creating it; I'm incredibly proud of it and it is up there with one of the best garments I've ever created! I felt so powerful wearing it and had the best night in London.

The pink tulle was sourced from my practice garment for the final of *The Great British Sewing Bee*. I made a mock-up for the final dress that didn't fit right and wasn't finished – I reused the metres of pink tulle in this dress, so it wasn't just sitting in a bag. However, I know that not everyone will just happen to have 10 metres of pink tulle sitting around spare, and you may not want to buy this polyester fabric brand new, and that's okay, but it's also okay if you do want to. See the section "Tips for Tulle" on page 168 for more info and sewing tips on this fabric. Don't rush with tulle; this dress calls for plenty of sewing time, but it's worth the hard work.

If you couldn't tell, this dress is heavily inspired by Villanelle (pink tulle all the way) and the design took many forms before the final one; see "A Note on Designing" (page 141) for a bit more info. I paired it with red shoes I already own, gold jewellery and a gold bag with pink and red designs on it that brought it all together.

This skirt is made from a lining cotton layer and 8 tulle layers. The top tulle layer has ruffles sewn onto the hem. These ruffles also feature on the bodice and add that extra oomph to the dress that it needed. You'll hate them by the time you're done sewing this dress!

Additional tools needed: patience for these damn ruffles

Patterns needed: bodice block

Techniques learned: gathering, tulle, layers, making bias binding, invisible zip

Seam allowances: 1.5cm unless otherwise stated

NOTION LIST:
- Matching thread (lots)
- Bias binding – make your own, see "Build from the Basics" (page 40)
- Concealed zip, at least 22cm long
- Hook and eye

MAKING THE TOP PATTERN

FRONT BODICE

1. Measure 6cm down from centre neck and draw line straight across
2. Measure 15cm down the side seam from underarm and draw line straight across – dispose of bottom section
3. Add seam allowance onto new seams that you have created (red lines in image)

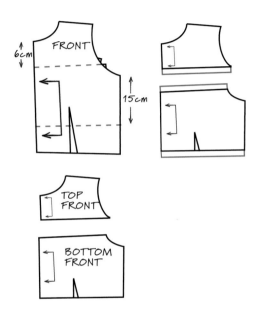

BACK BODICE

1. Measure 11cm down from centre neck and draw line straight across
2. Measure 15cm down the side seam from underarm and draw line straight across – dispose of bottom section
3. Add seam allowance onto new seams that you have created (red lines in image)

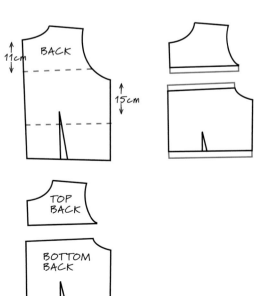

BIAS BINDING

4cm x approximately 30cm for each neck and armhole binding

SKIRT

For all skirt layers, you will have to sew widths together to get the total width you need. Ensure each layer has a centre back seam.

UNDERSKIRT
- Width about 2x your waist measurement (doesn't need to be exact) (150cm)
- Length (length needed + 1.5cm seam allowance at waist seam + hem allowance) (Mine is 55cm long)

TULLE LAYERS
- Width 2x width of underskirt (3m)
- Length (unsewn) of underskirt (55cm)

Top Tip

When using expensive fabric, or even one that you have limited amounts of, spend time making toiles (these are basically practice garments). I make mock-ups for any major pattern alterations and trust me, it is worth it, especially when you are experimenting with design or tricky fabrics.

RUFFLES
- 10cm wide

I recommend cutting 10cm lengths of the full width of tulle

- Cut on the fold and then fold the strips in half again
- This will allow you to gather four layers of tulle at a time – which is what we want

PATTERN PIECES

TOP FRONT BODICE
☐ 1x tulle

BOTTOM FRONT BODICE
☐ 1x tulle
☐ 1x lining fabric

TOP BACK BODICE
☐ 1x tulle

BOTTOM BACK BODICE
☐ 2x tulle

SKIRT
☐ 1x lining skirt
☐ 8x tulle skirt layers

EXTRA BITS
☐ Many strips for ruffles
☐ 1x bias binding
☐ 1x strip for shoulder seam stabilising
  - From cotton fabric, cut on grainline
  - 3cm x 1m

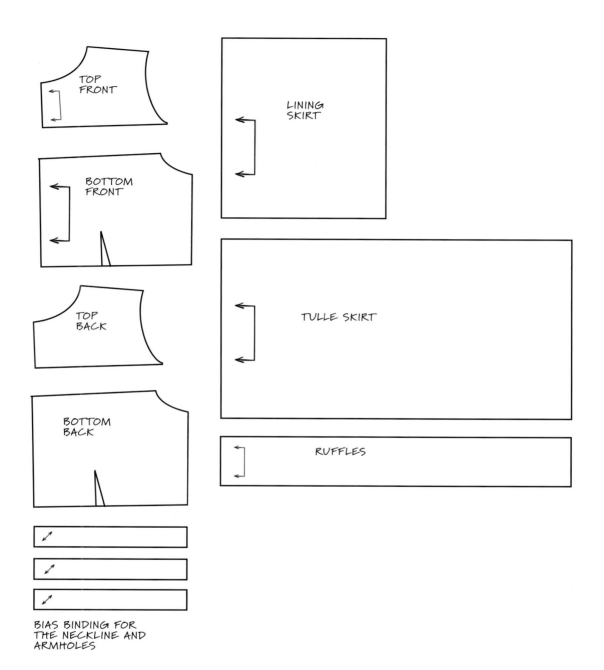

TOP FRONT

BOTTOM FRONT

TOP BACK

BOTTOM BACK

LINING SKIRT

TULLE SKIRT

RUFFLES

BIAS BINDING FOR THE NECKLINE AND ARMHOLES

SEWING THE DRESS

PREPARING THE BODICE

1. Sew darts into bottom front bodice and bottom back bodice
2. Baste tulle bottom front and bottom back onto respective lining pieces – now you will treat these as one layer
3. For both the front and back pieces, sew top bodice onto bottom bodice, finish edges and topstitch so seam is hidden by lining fabric
4. Create strip for stabilisation of bodice shoulder seams: fold right sides together and sew with 1cm seam allowance down length. Trim seam allowance and press open in middle of strip, turn inside out, and press flat with seam allowance open in middle of strip. These will be easier to turn inside out if you cut the strip into the lengths you need first (you need 2 shoulder seam lengths)
5. Sew shoulder seams (right sides together), trim seam allowance and stabilise with strip of cotton fabric by pinning the strip on the seam on the inside. Topstitch strip down a few mm away from shoulder seam line on either side of the seam
6. Sew side seams right sides together, finish and topstitch towards back bodice
7. Finish armhole edges with bias binding (see page 40), using method that removes 1cm from seam

PREPARING THE RUFFLES

8. Cut many ruffles – they will be 10cm wide by approximately 40cm long – comprised of four layers of folded fabric
9. Sew one row of gathering stitches in the middle of the ruffle using same coloured thread as dress (you will not be able to remove these at the end, so the thread must match). Gather each ruffle down to approximately 15cm
10. Pin a row of ruffles into place onto the top of the bodice, 2cm away from where the cotton fabric ends and leaving 1.5cm free at centre back for the zip
10. We will sew the bottom layer of bodice ruffle on once the skirt is attached
11. Stitch directly on top of the gathering stitches to secure the ruffle onto the fabric. Cut any stray thread

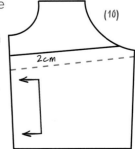

PREPARING THE SKIRT

12. Finish edges of back seam of underskirt
13. Sew back seam of underskirt, leaving 20cm open at the top for the zip
14. Sew side seams if needed, finish and press open
15. Hem underskirt (1.5cm allowance)
16. Sew tulle layers together as needed to get the width required of the skirt. Trim seam allowance down to a few millimetres

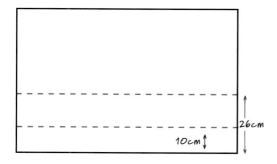

16. Prepare top tulle layer: sew ruffles onto bottom hem, one row 10cm away from edge and another 26cm away from edge. Stitch directly on top of the gathering stitches to secure the ruffle onto the fabric. Cut any stray thread
18. Sew the back seams of all eight tulle layers, leaving 25cm open at top, using as small a seam allowance as you can, or a 1cm seam allowance, and trim down to a few mm
19. Baste the tulle layers together at the waist
20. Gather tulle layers together down to width of underskirt, leaving 1.5cm free at centre back edge for zip. Stitch onto underskirt at 1.2cm

CONSTRUCTING THE DRESS

21. Gather all skirt layers down to width of bodice
22. Stitch onto bodice at waist seam right sides together, finish seam and topstitch seam to bodice, doing an extra line of stitching 1cm away from seam
23. Remove all basting stitches
24. Sew bottom row of bodice ruffles on, stitching 2cm above waist seam and leaving 1.5cm free at centre

back for zip. Stitch directly on top of the gathering stitches to secure the ruffle onto the fabric. Cut any stray thread
25. Sew invisible zip in (see page 171)
26. Sew bias binding onto neck edge using method that removes 1cm; fold edges in by 1cm at zip edge to finish them
27. Add hook and eye onto top of bodice

TIPS FOR TULLE

Tulle is an incredibly versatile, useful and unique fabric to use. It is fantastic fabric to play around with and create new shapes and volume.

It's definitely not the most sustainable fabric since it is 100% polyester, but there is nothing affordable quite like it that allows you the same creative freedom that tulle does. The trickiness when using tulle comes from the fact that one layer is so thin it can become almost invisible sometimes.

Here are some other tips for using tulle fabric that I find useful for making the process easier.

ORGANISING

Tulle pieces often end up being very similar-looking rectangles. Keep track of your layers and stay organised by labelling pieces with small pieces of paper safety-pinned into them, so you know what all the rectangles are for.

PRESSING

Since the fabric is polyester, you can't use high heat when pressing. I recommend avoiding pressing where possible during this project. I topstitch seams instead, since they are basically all covered by ruffles anyway. The seams of the tulle skirt layers don't need to be pressed or topstitched since they are so slim.

HEMMING

Tulle fabric has an incredible feature – it doesn't need to be hemmed! This means you can use metres upon metres of it without needing to hem it, saving you countless hours. It also means you need to make sure the cuts you make in the tulle are sharp and clean, since they will be visible in the end garment. Good quality fabric scissors needed here.

PINNING

When basting layers of tulle together, pins just get lost in the fabric and tend to fall out. It is much easier to use sewing clips for this process. They are cheap and easily bought online or in sewing shops. When using the cotton lining during this project, pins will be absolutely fine.

INVISIBLE ZIP GUIDE

(2)

(4)

(6)

(7)

(9)

(10)

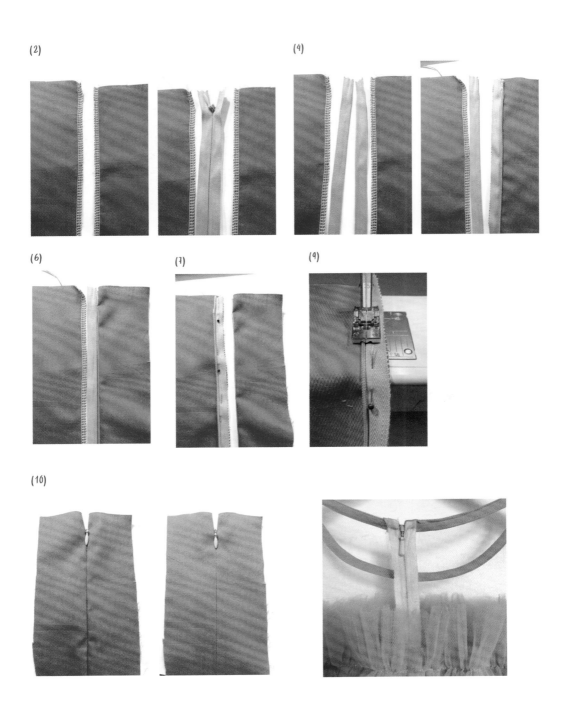

INVISIBLE ZIP INSERTION

Sewing in an invisible zip is quite a technical skill. It is made much easier by the invention of the invisible (or concealed) zip foot. This honestly changed the game for me. Being able to insert an invisible zip is a great skill to have, as it gives garments a professional and clean look.

Stitch the seam until it is 5cm away from where the bottom of the zip will end up (1)

Finish the edges of the seam and press it open. If you want, you can use chalk to mark 1.5cm from the edges of this seam (2)

Gently press the zip teeth open with a low heat iron (3)

Open your zip and pin the right side of your zip to the right side of the fabric, with the top of the tape matching the top of your fabric and the zip teeth at the 1.5cm seam allowance mark (4)

Baste in place (5)

Sew with invisible zip foot from top until the zip pull prevents you sewing more (6)

Without twisting the zip, pin the left side of your zip to the left side of the fabric, with the top of the tape matching the top of your fabric and the zip teeth at the 1.5cm seam allowance mark. Make sure the end of the zip matches the right side you have already sewn on (7)

Baste in place (8)

Sew with invisible zip foot from top until the zip pull prevents you sewing more (9)

Press the finished zip (10)

Using a normal zip foot, stitch the gap in the seam below zip. When you get close to the zip it can be hard to keep to the seam allowance, so I recommend closing the gap with hand stitches (11)

CHAPTER 10

THE
60s DRESS

FIRST THINGS FIRST

This dress has a strong 60s vibe which, although it isn't a style I've explored before, I love. The blue reminded me of the parachute dress I made during *The Great British Sewing Bee* – which was a colour I unexpectedly was attracted to – and I wanted a dress with impact, volume and colour, so the blue was perfect.

This whole dress is built from simple alterations to a bodice block – making it a great project for beginners that looks complex and put together at the end. You can really alter this pattern to fit your ideal design – add more length to the bottom ruffle, or less, make it maxi, make the collar slimmer so it isn't turtleneck, or make the whole thing a top rather than a dress. Do whatever you fancy!

This ideal fabric for this pattern is a lightweight non-stretch fabric. You can choose one that has drape to it, such as a viscose, or a stiffer fabric, such as cotton lawn, to create a more structured look.

Patterns needed: bodice block

Techniques learned: burrito method, gathering

Seam allowances: 1.5cm unless otherwise stated

NOTION LIST:
- Matching thread
- Interfacing for facing pieces
- Rolled hem foot (optional)

MAKING THE PATTERN

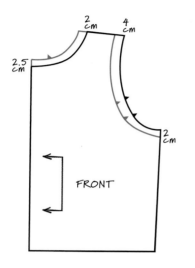

MAKING THE ADJUSTED FRONT BODICE

Start with the basic bodice block.

1. Remove 2cm from side seam at armhole
2. Remove 4cm from armhole edge at shoulder seam
3. Form new armhole with smooth curve – keep notches same
4. Add 2.5cm onto front neck
5. Add 2cm onto neck edge at shoulder seam
6. Form new neck edge with smooth curve – make notch 6.5cm from centre front

MAKING THE FRONT FACING

Use the adjusted front bodice.

1. Mark 7cm down from armhole
2. Mark 10cm down from neck
3. Join line from front neck to side seam – flattening the curve when reaching either end
4. Mark notch on neck edge, 6.5cm from centre front

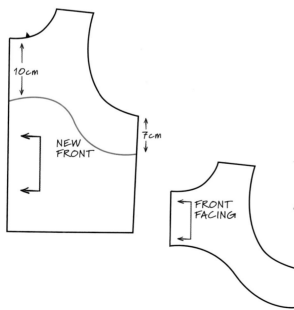

MAKING THE FRONT DRESS PATTERN

Start with the adjusted front bodice.

1. Make parallel cuts in pattern as seen in diagram. When cutting towards the shoulder seam do not cut through but leave a few mm so you are able to pivot these pieces while they are still attached to each other
2. Add 6.5cm volume between centre front edge and notch (or as much as desired)
3. Pivot pattern at shoulder seam until front hem length = 64cm
   - This can be adjusted for amount of volume wanted in the dress, pivot more for more volume or pivot less for less volume
4. Add 35cm onto bottom of bodice, to extend side seam to 60.5cm
   - This can be adjusted easily for how tall you are and how long you want the dress to be
5. Mark notch 23.5cm from top of side seam
   - This is where we will be placing our pocket pieces

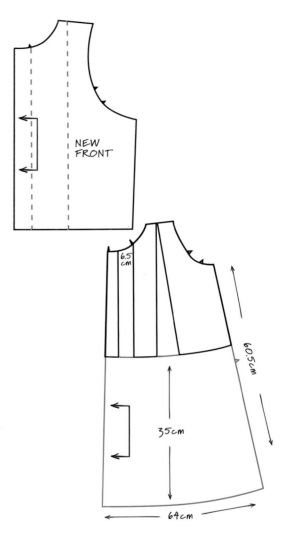

MAKING THE ADJUSTED BACK BODICE

1. Remove 2cm from side seam at armhole
2. Remove 4cm from armhole edge at shoulder seam
3. Form new armhole with smooth curve – keep notches same
4. Add 1cm onto front neck
5. Add 1cm onto neck edge at shoulder seam
6. Form new neck edge with smooth curve
7. Remove 1.5cm from centre back edge (we're making a pattern on the fold)

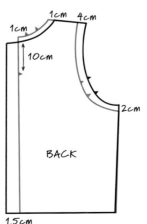

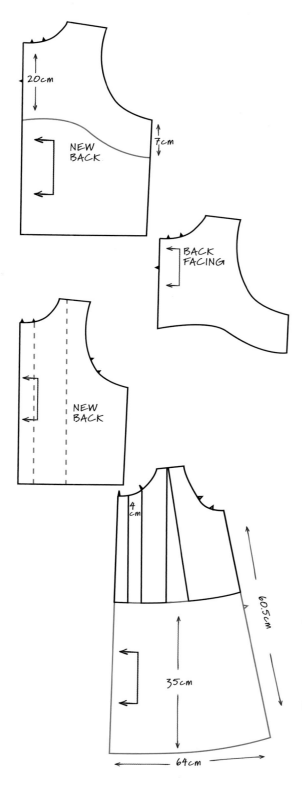

8. Mark a notch 10cm down centre back and one on neck edge, 1cm in from centre back
9. Mark another notch on neck edge, 6cm from centre back

MAKING THE BACK FACING

1. Mark 7cm down from armhole
2. Mark 20cm down from centre back neck
3. Join line from front neck to side seam – flattening the curve when reaching either end

MAKING THE BACK DRESS PATTERN

1. Make parallel cuts in pattern as seen in diagram. When cutting towards the shoulder seam do not cut through but leave a few mm so you are able to pivot these pieces while they are still attached to each other
2. Add 4cm volume between centre back edge and notch (or as much as wanted)
3. Pivot pattern at armhole until back hem length is 64cm
   - This can be adjusted for amount of volume wanted in the dress, pivot more for more volume or pivot less for less volume
4. Add 35cm onto bottom of bodice, to extend side seam to 60.5cm
   - This can be adjusted easily for how tall you are and how long you want the dress to be
5. Mark notch 23.5cm from top of side seam
   - This is where we will be placing our pocket pieces

RUFFLE.

I wanted my ruffle to be roughly twice the volume so made it 500cm long and 18.5cm wide. Yours should be 2x the length of your dress hem and as wide as needed to make the dress the length you want. You will need to piece rectangles of fabric together to get a length long enough.

COLLAR

- Again, you might need to piece rectangles of fabric together to get a length long enough.
- 12.5cm x 214cm

STEPS

1. Create a point during sewing steps
2. Create notch at centre front
3. Measure the total length of neck edge on pattern pieces, remove 2cm from this measurement
   - E.g. for me total neck edge is 50cm, remove 2cm = 48cm
4. Half this measurement
   - E.g. 24cm for me
5. Take the final measurement from step 4, measure this distance from the centre neck and create a notch at this point. Repeat on both sides

PATTERN PIECES

- ☐ 1x front dress on fold
- ☐ 1x back dress on fold
- ☐ 1x front facing on fold and interfacing
- ☐ 1x back facing on fold and interfacing
- ☐ 1x ruffle
- ☐ 1x collar
- ☐ 4x side seam pockets (remember to cut 2x mirrored pairs)

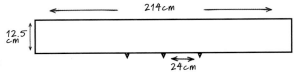

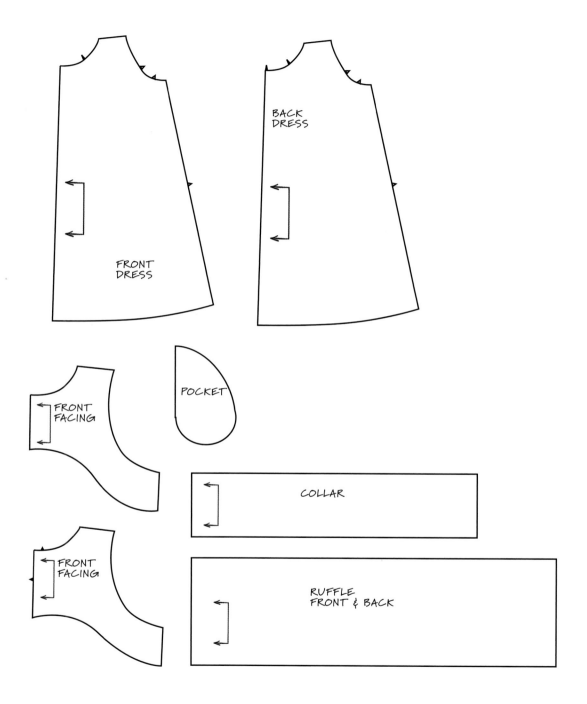

BACK
DRESS

FRONT
DRESS

FRONT
FACING

POCKET

FRONT
FACING

COLLAR

RUFFLE
FRONT & BACK

SEWING THE DRESS

PREPARING THE DRESS

1. Stay stitch all necklines and armholes of dress pieces
2. Finish curved edges of pockets
3. Stitch straight edges of pocket onto side seams, (right sides together) with 1cm seam allowance, bottom of pocket meeting notch on side seam
4. Finish side seam edges
5. Press seam towards pocket, understitch seam onto pocket
6. Sew shoulder seam right sides together, finish, and press open
7. On the back dress, draw a triangle at the centre back, using the notches as the points of the triangle
8. Gather front and back neck edges between notches

(7)

SEWING ON THE FACING

9. Attach interfacing to facing pieces
10. Finish lower edges of facing and side seams
12. Pin necklines of dress and facing together, right sides together, and stitch only the triangle at the centre back following the lines you drew on step 7
13. Cut down the middle of the triangle you have sewn, getting as close to the point as possible
14. Turn right sides out and press flat
15. Baste neck edges of dress and facing together (wrong side together) making gathers even along neck edges
16. One armhole at a time – take right side of facing and wrap it around dress (sandwiching dress in the middle) to pin to right side of dress armhole. (This is called the Burrito method)

(15)

(16)

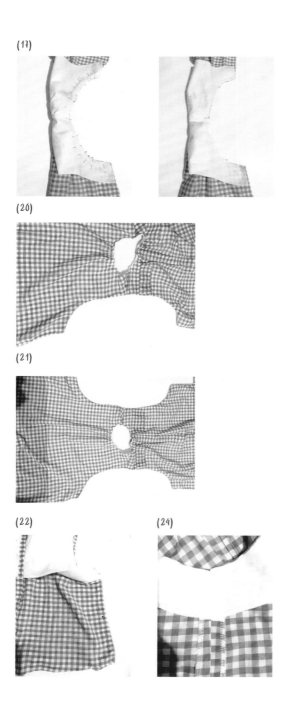

(17)

(20)

(21)

(22)

(24)

17. Stitch this seam, trim and clip seam allowance
18. Turn dress to right side through gap
19. Understitch this seam where possible, stitching seam allowance to facing
    - Start at either edge of armhole and go towards shoulder seam, you may not fully reach the shoulder seam due to the small opening and that's fine
20. Press armhole edge
21. Repeat steps 16–19 for the other armhole
    - You will now have two finished arm-holes

SEWING THE SIDE SEAMS

22. Pin side seams together of facing and dress right sides together – making sure to match armhole seams up
23. Stitch side seams, from edge of facing to top notch of pockets, rotate dress to sew around curved edge until you meet the side seam again, add back stitches. Restart stitching side seam where bottom pocket notch is and carry on until hem
24. Clip back dress seam allowance above pocket to allow you to press seam open above level of the pocket
25. Press pocket and seam allowance below pocket to front of dress
26. Hang the dress up for at least 24 hours before sewing ruffle on; this is to allow the side seams to drop, since they are sewn on the bias. In the meantime, work on the collar and preparing the ruffle.

SEWING ON THE COLLAR

27. Fold collar piece in half right sides together
28. Stitch collar from side notch to point on both sides, leaving gap unsewn in middle of collar between the notches
29. Trim and clip seam allowances, turn and press
30. Pin one free edge of collar to neck edge, matching centre front notches, leave two cm of spare unsewn collar on either side of the neck edge – this allows you to fully pin collar onto neck
31. Stitch neck edge onto collar, trim and clip seam, press seam towards collar
32. Fold other collar edge down over raw edges and slip stitch shut
    - You can topstitch this if you want visible stitching. If you are doing this, I recommend topstitching all around the collar edge

SEWING ON THE RUFFLE

33. Prepare ruffle – sew pieces together to create full length needed. Finish seam allowance and press seams open
34. Hem ruffle – I used a rolled hem foot
35. Gather top edge down to length of dress hem
36. Once dress has dropped, even out the hemline; the side seams should have dropped. I had to cut 2.5cm off each side seam. Grade this to centre front/back to make hem straight
37. Sew on ruffle to dress with right sides together, finish edge and press upwards

(28)

(29)

(30)   (32)

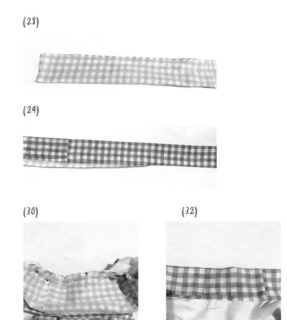

Top Tip

When creating a rolled hem on a long loop of fabric (e.g. a ruffle), I find it easier to sew the hem while the loop is open. Sew your pieces together along the seams apart from one, leaving you with a long strip of fabric. Now hem the long strip using a rolled hem foot. After this you can sew the remaining seam shut, ensuring the hems are matched up well. This is easier than trying to do a rolled hem on a loop of fabric!

A LITTLE EXTRA

You can easily turn this dress pattern into a top. All you need to do is stop the pattern at the waist and hem the bottom edge instead of adding a ruffle. You can even make this a refashioning project like I did!

CHAPTER 11

BAGS

Bags are fantastic projects for using up second-hand clothing. You have an opportunity to use fabrics you wouldn't normally and create a statement piece. I enjoyed combining different colours and patterns in these projects to create bold and graphic designs.

In the upcoming projects, I have created four very different styles of bags. These create foundations of patterns for you to experiment with. They all have different scopes of use: some are more casual and perfect for shopping, while others could be made in more opulent fabrics and dressed up. Get creative by combining fabrics and adding your own features such as pockets or ruffles.

A few logistical notes for this chapter. All seam allowances are 1cm unless stated otherwise. If you are using fabrics or clothes that are on the lighter side, interface them with heavy-weight interfacing to stiffen them. When doing this, don't interface the seam allowance of the pattern pieces; this saves the seams from becoming bulky and unmanageable.

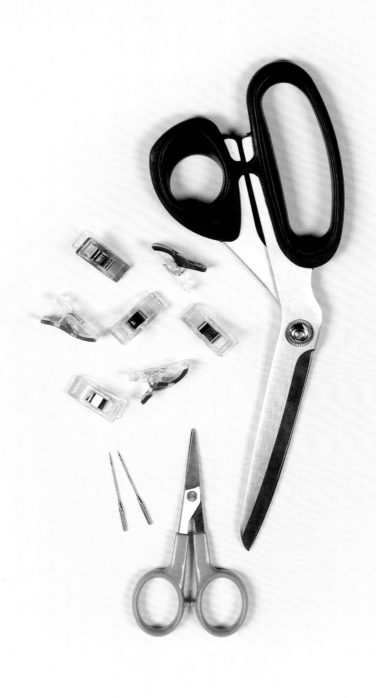

HOW TO USE HEAVIER FABRIC

Bags often need more structure in order to keep their shape and hold the weight of different items. This means the fabrics we will be using in this chapter are thicker than the rest of the book. They're nothing difficult, like using thick leather, but heavier fabrics can be trickier to work with, and we can still take some steps to make it easier for ourselves.

So here are some tips to help you on your way.

USE THE CORRECT NEEDLE SIZE

I cannot emphasise enough how important it is to use the correct needle size. For thicker fabrics you will need a size like 90/14 or 100/16. These needles have a pointier tip to get through the thick layers of fabric. It's no good using a needle made for viscose on 10oz denim; all you will do is damage your machine.

USE SEWING CLIPS

Thick fabrics can be tough to push pins through. Avoid hurting your fingers by using sewing clips instead. These are cheap and easy to find in sewing shops or online. They're a really useful replacement for when pins aren't suitable – or use them all the time in place of pins if you prefer.

TRIM SEAM ALLOWANCES

Heavy fabrics create bulky seams. Often with a 1cm seam allowance I will skip the trimming step, but not for heavy fabrics. The bulk can build up quickly, especially if you are adding a lining. Trim seams down to about 5mm.

TOPSTITCH SEAMS

If seams are not pressing well because of their bulkiness, try to topstitch them instead. Press as much as you can without damaging the fabrics and then take them to the machine to get a clean look. If you find you need to topstitch to control the fabric, consider topstitching seams throughout the whole project to make it a feature – you could even use contrasting thread!

CIRCLE BAG

I adore this circle-shaped shoulder bag. It is fully lined, has loads of space and is made from old clothes. The strap length allows it to be worn on your shoulder, while the placement of it means the bag is closed without having an official closure, giving it a bit more security.

To take this project further, you could add pockets to the outside of the bag, or to the lining. Play around with the size of the straps to create different styles.

Ideally you want to find a heavy fabric for the outer bag. I used a pair of yellow denim jeans that I had to interface so the fabric would be stiff enough. For the lining fabric, you can use a lightweight fabric such as cotton poplin. I used a fabric remnant my mum gave me that is covered in lemons and oranges. I thought it paired perfectly with the yellow denim.

Seam allowances: 1cm unless otherwise stated

NOTION LIST:
- Matching thread
- Interfacing for all outer pieces

MAKING THE PATTERN

CIRCLE

1. Draft a circle with a radius of 20cm
2. Mark a centre top and centre bottom notch
3. Measure 9cm from centre top at either side and mark notches for the strap placement
4. Measure a further 9cm from strap notches and mark notches for end of base placement
5. Measure 5cm from centre bottom at either side and mark notches for gap

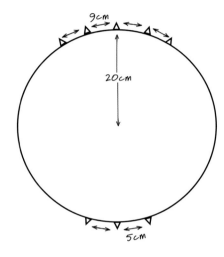

> These measurements include all seam allowances (1cm throughout pattern)

RECTANGLE FOR BASE OF BAG

8cm x 92cm

STRAPS

8cm x 70cm

PATTERN PIECES

- ☐ 2x body for outer bag – cut from thighs of jeans
- ☐ 2x body for lining bag
- ☐ 2x body for interfacing bag if needed
- ☐ 1x outer base – piece shorter lengths together as needed
- ☐ 1x lining base
- ☐ 1x interfacing base if needed
- ☐ 2x straps – piece shorter lengths together as needed

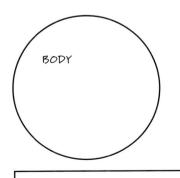

SEWING THE BAG

(3)

(5)

(7)

(9)

(10)

1. Interface wrong side of outer fabrics for circle and base pieces
2. Cut 1cm off the lining base piece at one of the short ends
3. Place right sides of outer and lining base pieces together
4. Sew only the short seams on either end
5. Press open and trim the seam allowance of the outer fabric down to a few mm
6. Turn the base right sides out, so that the wrong sides of the fabric are touching. Roll the seam of the short end towards the lining by 5mm
7. Topstitch the short ends and baste the long ends together
8. Make straps by pressing long edges of pieces in by 1cm and pressing the whole length in half again. Topstitch down both long edges
9. Place one outer circle piece down, right side facing up. Pin base onto this, right sides together following notches, and placing middle of base to centre bottom notch. Pin strap into place as per right image. Straps need to be pinned horizontally with the notch on the bag sitting in the middle of the strap. Stitch the base and straps in place the whole way around the circle at 8mm
10. Place a circle lining piece on top of this, right sides together. Pin this in place, leaving a 10cm gap at the bottom of the circle, guided by the notches

11. Sew around the circle, again leaving the 10cm gap open at the bottom of the circle as per notches
12. Except the gap – trim the seam allowance down to 5mm and clip triangles into seam allowance
13. Turn right sides out through gap at bottom
14. Press this seam flat
15. Press lining seam allowance of gap in (1cm) and hand stitch this gap closed
16. Topstitch around whole circle
17. Place unsewn outer circle right side up
18. Pin straps on as per step 9
19. Pin other side of base onto circle, right sides together, tucking in the straps so they don't get caught in any more sewing
20. Stitch whole way around circle at 8mm
21. Place remaining lining piece on top of the bag, right side facing down. Pin around circle edge leaving 10cm gap at bottom as per notches
22. Repeat steps 11–16

(11)

(16)

(19)

(20)

(21)

CUBE BAG

This cube bag is a very simple, small handbag, and the addition of scrunched handles adds a cute detail. The pink denim I used suited the vibe of the pattern! There are additional instructions for adding a popper on the top of the bag, to allow extra closure and safety, but that's not essential for the finished product.

To take this project further, you could add pockets to the lining. Play around with the length and width of the strap fabric to create different scrunchie effects. This bag could definitely be made for an occasion if the right fabric is used, such as a brocade for a more luxurious end result.

Ideally you want to find a heavy fabric for the outer bag. I used a pair of pink denim jeans and stiffened the fabric with interfacing (I didn't interface the strap fabric since it was being scrunched). For the lining fabric, you can use a lightweight fabric such as cotton poplin. I used a fabric remnant I already had, which happened to match the pink denim to a T!

Seam allowances: 1cm unless otherwise stated

NOTION LIST:
- Matching thread
- 2.5cm wide elastic, 70cm long (You could also use wide ribbon for this, but I chose elastic as it was thicker)
- Popper (optional)
- Interfacing for all outer pieces if needed

MAKING THE PATTERN

OUTER BAG

- 1x long strip from outer fabric
- 2x side square from outer fabric
- 4x outer fabric facing

outer fabric

x1 — 53 cm

19cm

x2 — 19cm — 19cm

x4 — 6cm

LINING FABRIC

- 1x long lining strip
- 2x square side lining pieces

STRAPS

- 2x 8cm x 50cm

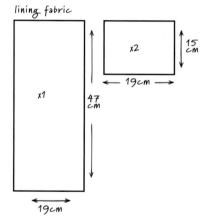

lining fabric

x1 — 47 cm

19cm

x2 — 15 cm — 19cm

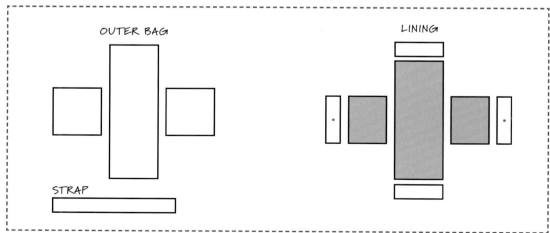

OUTER BAG   LINING

STRAP

Pink: lining fabric   *White:* outer fabric   *Pink dot:* popper placement

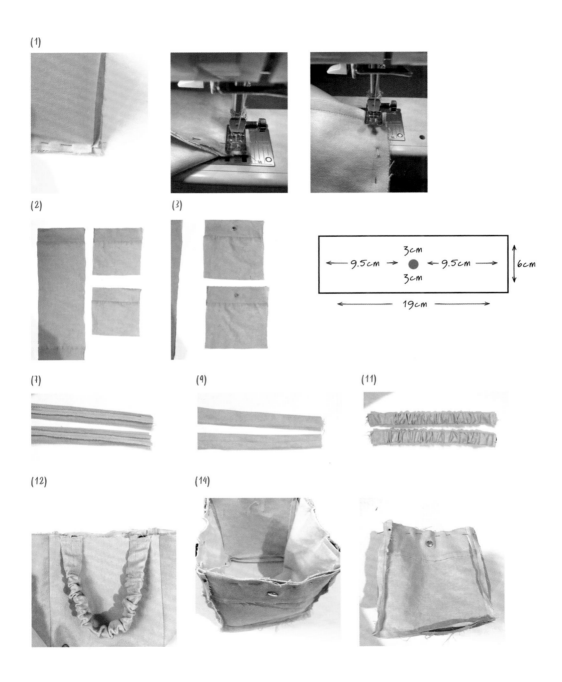

(1)

(2) (3)

3cm
←— 9.5cm —→ ● ←— 9.5cm —→ 6cm
3cm
←——— 19cm ———→

(7) (9) (11)

(12) (14)

SEWING THE BAG

1. Prepare outer bag by sewing long edges of middle strip around three edges of square pieces, right sides together. Make snips in the long strip where it meets the corners of the square piece to help you pin and sew. When sewing, sew with the square piece on the top and pivot the fabric in the machine (with the needle in the down position) to help you sew around the corners

2. Sew facings to lining fabrics and press seams towards lining

3. If you want to, add a popper in the middle of the facings. Follow instructions on your packet of poppers for this. Add a popper to two of your four facings and use these facings to create the square pieces. Add the top section to one side and the bottom section to the other, ensuring the popper will close with the right sides of the fabrics together. The long strip for the lining bag will not have a popper on

4. Sew lining main strip onto square pieces as per the outer bag, make sure to match up the facing seams. On ONE side, leave a gap in the lining fabric unsewn (about 10cm) on the middle straight edge

5. Prepare straps by folding in half, right sides together, along long edge

6. Sew long edge only

7. Trim seam allowance and press flat in middle of tube

8. Turn to right side

9. Press flat again, with seam allowance in middle of tube

10. Insert about 32cm elastic into this tube with a safety pin, securing the elastic down at either end – you can add more or less elastic to make straps longer or shorter

11. Sew elastic at either end at 7mm to secure

12. Sew straps onto outer bag, on the short ends of the long strip, making the edges of the strap sit 2cm away from the seams. One strap should be sewn onto the same side of the long strip at two points to make a loop

13. Place outer bag inside lining bag, right sides together

14. Pin outer bag to lining bag around the top edge, matching the seams

15. Sew all around edge, trim seam allowance

16. Turn the bag to the right side through the gap you left in the lining bag

17. Press the top seam flat and topstitch

18. Hand sew the gap in lining closed and push lining inside outer bag. You can add a few hand stitches at corners to secure lining inside bag, making sure they are hidden in the seams of the outer bag, so they remain invisible

TOTE BAG

Everyone always needs a tote bag. This one is a standard-size tote bag made from two different second-hand garments – giving you the opportunity to experiment with colours and patterns. I used a gingham men's shirt from a charity shop, and an old, embroidered skirt of mine that no longer fitted me.

You'll also learn a new skill: making a pocket with zip closure! This gives the bag a bit more security for your phone and other valuables. If you want to omit this feature, cut out two "back bags" and start sewing from step 12.

The weight of fabric needed depends on how you want the final bag to look. You could create a lighter weight tote bag that can be folded up and used as a shopping bag, or a heavier weight one for carrying around more things. Just make sure that your straps are thick enough – interface if needed – and that the fabrics used for your bag are of matching weight. For example, don't use a light fabric for the top section and heavy one for the bottom, you want the weights to match.

Techniques learned: creating a pocket with zip

Seam allowances: 1cm unless otherwise stated

NOTION LIST:
- Matching thread
- 20cm long zip – I used one with metal teeth that I had knocking about, but one with plastic teeth will do just fine
- Interfacing for all pieces necessary

ℓMAKING THE PATTERN

PATTERN PIECES

☐ Flower fabric = white
☐ Gingham fabric = pink
☐ Back of bag (cut 1 of each)
☐ Front of bag (cut 1 of each)
☐ Pocket pieces (cut 1 of each)
☐ Straps (cut 2 and interfacing)

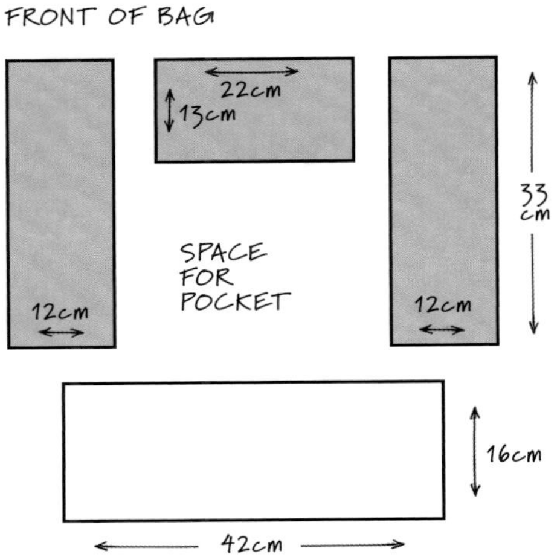

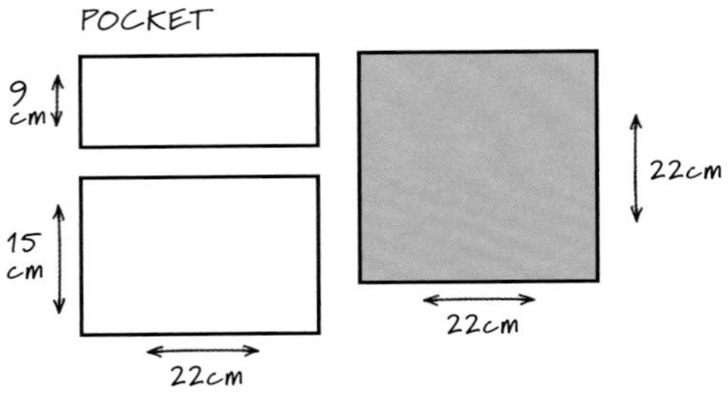

FRONT OF BAG

22cm

13cm

SPACE
FOR
POCKET

33 cm

12cm

12cm

16cm

42cm

POCKET

9 cm

15 cm

22cm

22cm

22cm

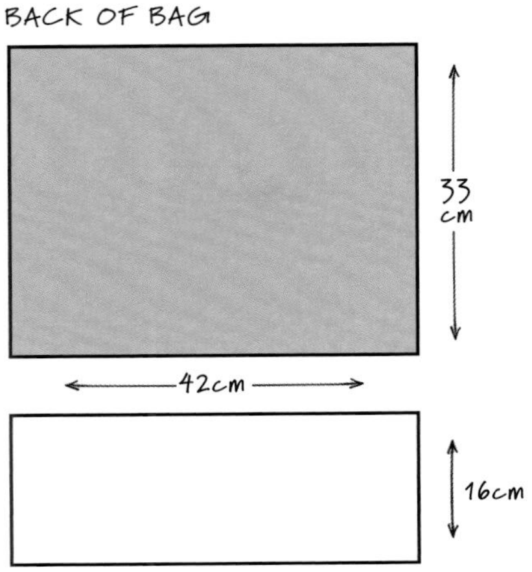

BACK OF BAG

33 cm

42cm

16cm

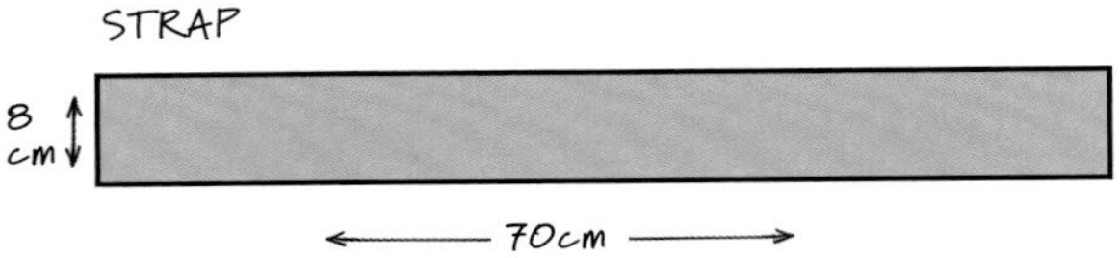

STRAP

8 cm

70cm

SEWING THE BAG

1. Interface pieces as needed

PREPARING THE POCKET

(2)

2. Lay pocket pieces out in front of you, right side up
3. Press edges of outer pocket pieces that are next to the zip. Press inward by 1cm
4. Pin them onto either side of the zip, sitting 2mm away from zip teeth
5. Topstitch these onto the zip tape using a zip foot to get close to the edges
6. Place this outer pocket piece on top of the pocket lining with wrong side of outer pocket touching right side of pocket lining and pin around all edges
7. Stitch around all four edges at 7mm

(3)

(4)

(5)

(6)

(7)

SEWING THE FRONT BAG

8. Lay pieces down in front of you, right sides up
9. Sew top of pocket piece onto rectangle above it right sides together. Finish seam and press upwards
10. Sew middle strip to two outer pieces right sides together. Finish seam and press outwards
11. Sew top piece onto bottom piece Right sides together. Finish seam and press down. Topstitch if needed

SEWING THE BAG BACK

12. Lay pieces down in front of you, right sides up
13. Sew top piece onto bottom piece right sides together. Finish seam and press down. Topstitch if needed

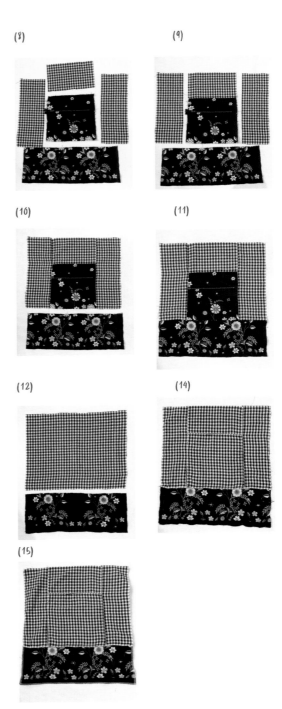

(16)

(17)

(21)

(23)

(24)

(26)

CONSTRUCTING THE BAG

14. Sew front bag to back bag around side and bottom edges, with right sides together

15. Finish seams and press to back bag as much as you can

16. Create a flat base by pinning the side seams to the bottom seam at each corner

17. Measure 5cm down from point and draw a line straight across

18. Stitch across this line

19. Press this flap inside the bag and hand stitch it down to the bottom seam of the bag top to secure it

20. Prepare straps by folding long edges in by 1cm and then folding strap in half again. Topstitch down both long edges of strap

21. Pin strap to front of bag where the seams are, ensuring the strap is not twisted

22. Pin a strap to the back bag at the same points, using the front bag as a guide

23. Fold top edge inside by 1cm and press

24. Fold top edge in again by 2.5 cm and press. Pin around edge. Fold the strap back on itself so you can pin it to the edge

25. Sew two lines of stitches around top edge, one at 2mm and one at 2cm

26. At the straps, sew this square with cross design with plenty of back-stitching, to secure the straps

27. Turn bag to right side and give the seams a final press

KNOT BAG

This knot bag is the easiest bag in the book! No closures, zips or poppers needed; just four of the same pattern pieces. You could definitely dress up this bag for an occasion by using sparkly or more luxurious fabrics. It is worn on your arm by looping the short strap over the long one. I even like twisting the short strap once before looping it over, for a little extra tightness, but then maybe I'm just paranoid about losing things.

The bag is fully lined with no exposed seams, using a technique I learned on *The Great British Sewing Bee* (the dirty dancing dress)!

For this project you should use mid-weight fabric. I used second-hand cami tops that I interfaced with mid-weight interfacing. I chose to have polka dots for the outside of my bag, and a pop of colour with a bright green fabric for the lining. You won't be able to do the shopping with it, but it will be a great evening bag.

Seam allowances: 1cm unless otherwise stated

NOTION LIST:
- Matching thread
- Interfacing for all pieces necessary

PATTERN PIECES

☐ 2x outer bag
☐ 2x lining bag

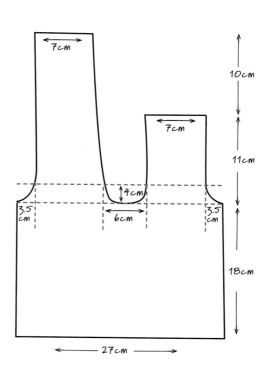

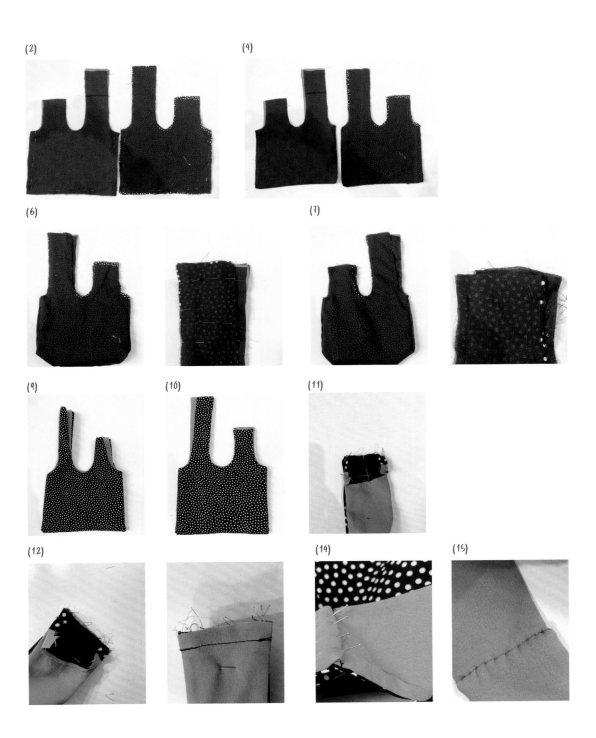

SEWING THE BAG

1. Interface pieces as needed – ensuring you end up with mirrored outer and lining pieces
2. For both outer bag and lining, place pieces on top of each other right sides together
3. Sew down the side seams and along bottom seam
4. Trim and clip seam allowances
5. Turn lining bag right side out and place into outer bag so that right sides are touching
6. Pin outer bag to lining bag along curved edges. At the four short ends, make sure to leave 1.5cm of seam unpinned as we will not be sewing this in order to form the straps
7. Sew around these edges, leaving that 1.5cm unsewn at all edges of the straps
8. Trim and clip all seam allowances
9. Turn bag to right side through one strap
10. Press the bag flat around all curved edges
11. At both the short strap and long strap, make sure the seam allowances of curved edges are folded in, pin the outer fabric of the strap right sides together. Add ONE lining strap layer to this, so you have three layers pinned together. Make sure to fold the other lining fabric back so you don't get it caught
12. Sew across strap through all three layers at 1cm seam allowance
13. Push this seam inside the remaining gap of the strap
14. With the remaining unsewn lining piece, fold the seam allowances inwards and pin in place
15. Hand stitch all remaining gap down with slip stitches (see page 47)
16. Repeat for the other strap

CHAPTER 12

ACCESSORIES

Making accessories is an amazing way to use up scraps and add interest to your outfit. I love using colourful scraps to make statement accessories like scrunchies and earrings. These are also great beginner projects or ones to do in groups since they could also be hand stitched. Some of my favourite memories with friends from university are from our craft club every Wednesday afternoon.

The best fabrics to use for all of these projects are lightweight non-stretch ones. You can use up scraps from the book projects so you can have matching accessories. All of the seam allowances in this chapter are 1cm unless otherwise stated.

SCRUNCHIES

Scrunchies are one of my favourite scrap projects and they are so easy! I love being able to match these with my outfit or wear a contrasting one. You can adjust the width and length of the fabric to make it bigger and bolder or keep it smaller and more contained – it is completely up to you.

These can be done on the machine or with hand sewing (if hand sewing, I recommend doing the bobble method as stitching the elastic needs to be very secure). On the machine they take minutes to stitch up.

Scrunchies can be made by two methods, either using a bobble or elastic. The latter is slightly easier.

You will need to cut a scrap of fabric 50cm x 12cm. You can adjust the length or width of this rectangle as you want. Making a thin scrunchie makes it look a bit more like a bracelet – cut a piece of fabric 50cm x 6cm and complete the steps as normal!

NOTION LIST:
- Bobble or elastic (I like using silicone bobbles as they are less likely to break, don't lose their strength and last longer)
- Elastic approx. 12cm long x 1cm wide
- Matching thread

BOBBLE METHOD

1. With right sides of fabric touching, fold in half and pin along the long edge of fabric, trapping the bobble on the inside, leaving 5cm of fabric unpinned at either end. You will need to bunch the fabric up around the bobble in order to pin along the whole length
2. Sew along this length, leaving 5cm unsewn at either end
3. Turn tube inside out around bobble
4. Sew short end of rectangle together right sides together – you will need to shimmy this seam while sewing to sew it, but it is possible
5. Close the opening by folding each side in by 1cm and pin
6. Either topstitch or hand stitch the opening closed

ELASTIC METHOD

1. With right sides touching, fold in half and pin along long edge of fabric leaving 5cm of fabric unpinned at either end
2. Sew along this length
3. Turn tube inside out
4. Sew short end together, right sides together
5. Cut the length of elastic you need; it should fit comfortably around your wrist with 1cm of overlap
6. Insert the elastic using a safety pin to shimmy it around the length of fabric (pin at the other end to keep it in place)
7. Overlap elastic by 1cm and stitch together securely
8. Close the opening by folding each side in by 1cm and pin
9. Either topstitch or hand stitch the opening closed

HEADBANDS

These are another of my favourite scrap projects. I find that headbands are the best way to keep my hair out of my face without getting a headache from a ponytail. They're great beginner projects with more scope for personalisation — you could add machine embroidery to the whole scrap piece or hand embroider patches onto the section that will be visible on the knot headband. They would also be a great project for kids to try!

NOTION LIST:
- Plastic headband — I buy mine online
- Matching thread

PATTERN PIECES

FOR GATHERED HEADBAND

BOTTOM PIECE
- Length of plastic headband + 2cm, for me 38cm
- Width of headband at widest point + 3cm, for example mine is 36cm by 3cm, so for me that's 6cm

TOP PIECE
- 1.5x length of plastic headband, for me 57cm
- Width of plastic headband plus 3cm, for me 6cm

FOR KNOT HEADBAND

CUT ONE RECTANGLE
- Length of plastic headband + 2cm, for example mine is 38cm
- Width of plastic headband at thickest point x 4, for example mine is 12cm

GATHERED HEADBAND

1. On the longer rectangle, place pins 10cm in from either short end on both long sides.
2. Gather the edges of the big rectangle between these pins
3. Gather down to length of small rectangle
4. Pin the rectangles right sides together and stitch long edges and one small edge
5. Trim and clip seam allowances
6. Turn this right side out
7. Insert plastic headband through open end
8. Fold the raw edge of the fabric on this end in by 1cm to conceal the headband, hand stitch this gap closed
9. Fold both long edges of the bottom of the headband inwards and hand stitch this down, in order to make the edges of the fabric as small as the plastic headband underneath

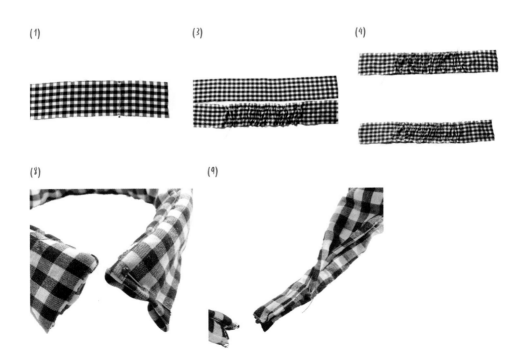

(1)

(3)

(4)

(8)

(9)

KNOT HEADBAND

1. Stitch rectangle right sides together along long edge
2. Press seam open, turn right sides out and press seam in middle of rectangle
3. Tie knot in middle of rectangle
4. Insert plastic headband through the knot so that the flat edge is on the underside of headband and the knot on the topside
5. At each end, finish short edges of fabric and fold up by 1cm, over plastic headband
6. Fold both long edges of the bottom of the headband inwards and hand stitch this down, in order to make the edges of the fabric as small as the plastic headband underneath

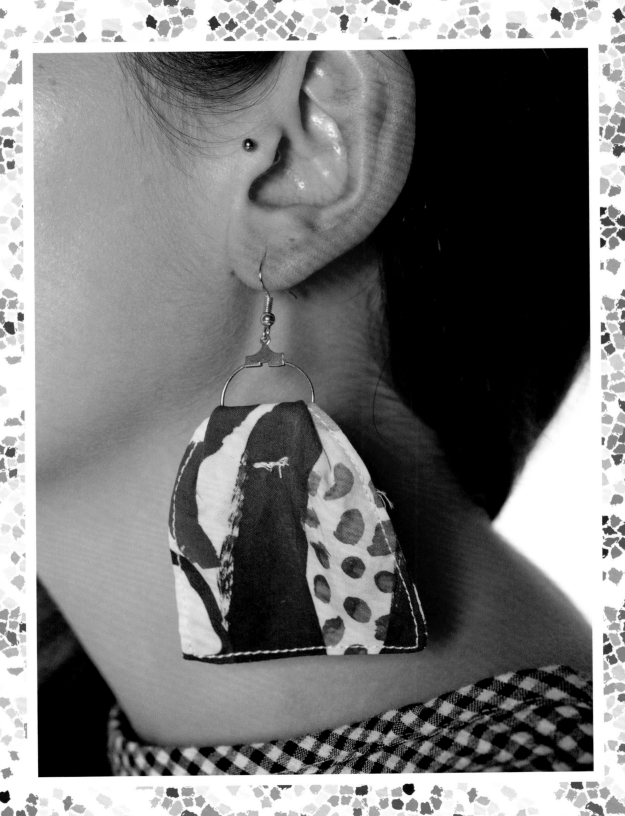

EARRINGS

Statement earrings are something I've fallen in love with over the past couple of years. They can really elevate an outfit and add a lot of detail. I've been slowly building my collection and creating my own is another way to do this. These are short projects using up teeny scraps and you will need to use some jewellery-making kit, but this is not too expensive. Get creative and use colourful fabrics for these, or even add trim for an even more dramatic look!

NOTION LIST:
- Earring hardware: hooks, hoops and jump rings
- Pair of small pliers

RUFFLE HOOP EARRINGS

1. Measure the circumference of your hoop
2. Cut out 2 rectangles that are 5cm wide and 1.5x the circumference of your hoop
3. Fold the rectangle in half along the long edge with right sides together
4. Sew around three edges, leaving 7mm free at each edge next to the fold

5. Trim and clip seam allowances
6. Turn to right side through one of the gaps, using a needle to help get pointy corners
7. Press flat
8. Stitch at 5mm away from folded edge along the whole piece – this creates a channel
9. Insert the hoop carefully into the channel and pull all of the way through

DROP TRIANGLE EARRINGS

1. Cut 4 rectangles 8cm x 10cm
2. Place 2 pieces right sides together and pin around edges
3. Sew around all edges, leaving a 2cm gap at one of the long edges
4. Trim and clip seam allowances
5. Turn right sides out, using a pin to help you get sharp corners
6. Press flat
7. Close gap with hand stitches or topstitching around whole edge
8. Create a pleat along one of the shorter ends as per the image:

9. Topstitch pleat in place
10. Fold the top of the pleat over a hoop attachment by 2cm
11. Sew a few stitches to secure the fabric over the hoop attachment
12. Using pliers, open the earring attachment, and secure it onto the hoop attachment

KNOT EARRINGS

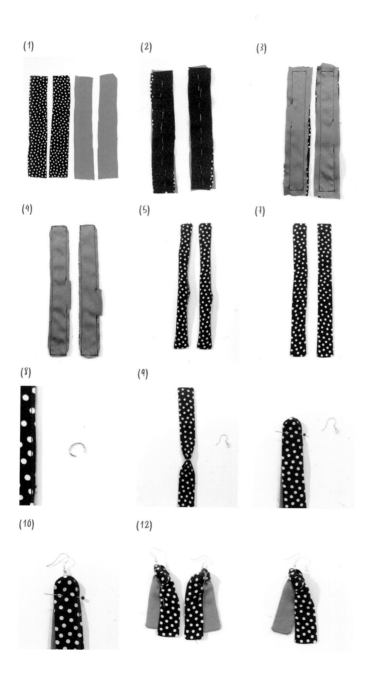

1. Cut 4 rectangles 22cm x 4cm. Interface two of these if you need to.
2. Pin two of the rectangles right sides together all the way around
3. Sew around all edges, leaving a 5cm gap at one of the long edges
4. Trim and clip seam allowances, leaving the unsewn seam allowance uncut
5. Turn right sides out, using a pin to help you get sharp corners
6. Press flat, with unsewn seam allowance folded in
7. Close gap with hand stitches or topstitching
8. Open a jump ring with a pair of pliers
9. Place this over the middle of the rectangle and close the jump ring with pliers
10. Use pliers to open the ring on the earring loop and place around jump ring
11. Tie the fabric into a knot, carefully pulling to create a nice shape
12. Sew a few hand stitches on the two tie ends to keep them together

JEANS REFASHION

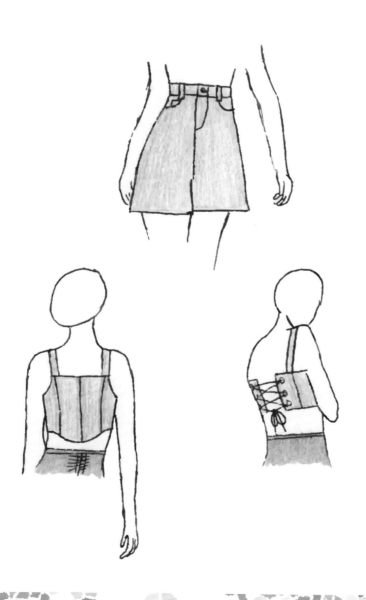

FIRST THINGS FIRST

This chapter is a more advanced refashioning project teaching you how to take an old pair of jeans and turn it into a cute pair of summer shorts with a matching 90s corset-style top. The jeans you use should fit you around the waist and hips in a style you like (high-waisted or mid-rise etc.), and the legs should be either straight or wide, just not skinny as they won't have enough fabric. The denim should not be stretchy.

This top is a more technical variation of the crop top project on page 55, and I would recommend making that top before trying this one to ensure you have good foundation skills you can build upon.

With a lace-up back, boning, fully lined bodice and topstitching features, this corset-style top is packed full of new skills to learn. It is easy to fit and there are multiple ways you could personalise both the shorts and top, such as adding decorating topstitching, dyeing the fabric, or adding trims. Get creative!

The boning channels can be created from either ribbons or bias binding. Topstitching is optional but I think it adds a nice feature detail for the denim fabric. I chose to use gold topstitching thread to match the original one used in the jeans.

For tips on sewing with heavy fabric, see page 189.

Patterns needed: bodice block

Techniques learned: using boning, creating channel, making and sewing bias binding

Seam allowances: 1.5cm unless otherwise stated

NOTION LIST:
- Matching thread
- Bias binding – make your own, see "Build from the Basics" (page 40)
- Ribbon/bias binding for boning channels – 3cm wide and about 2m long
- 1cm wide boning, about 2m long
- Topstitch thread (optional)
- Eyelets and tools to use these (should be 11mm wide)
- Small rectangle of interfacing to reinforce eyelets

SEWING THE SHORTS

This is the easy part of the project! Use a pair of shorts you already own to know how long you want your new shorts to be.

1. Place shorts you already own on top of your pair of jeans
2. Trace the hem length, adding on hem allowance (I recommend adding 2cm)
3. Cut both jean legs on this line
4. Create a double-fold hem by folding in 1cm twice
5. Topstitch hem at 8mm
6. Use the legs you cut off to create your top!

A NOTE ON BONING

Boning is placed in garments to add structure. You can get many types of boning, including plastic and steel.

I tend to use plastic boning as it is cheap, easily accessible and requires no additional tools to use. All you need to do is grade the corners of the cut pieces and file the sharp edges down before using it.

Steel boning provides a bit more support but requires more intense toolwork to use.

MAKING THE TOP PATTERN

Follow instructions in the project on page 82 to create a new front and back bodice with square neck pattern alteration.

Strat with square neckline bodice.

1. Create centre front and side front by continuing line of dart to neckline, separating pieces, removing the space where the dart sits
2. Add seam allowance onto either side (1.5cm) of the seam you created
3. Repeat for back bodice to create side back and centre back
4. Create curve for front (optional)
   - Take 2.5cm length off the back pieces
   - Take 2.5cm length off the side seam and grade this into the existing hem to create a nice curve
5. Make a notch midway on the side seam of side front and side back to help you orientate similar looking pieces

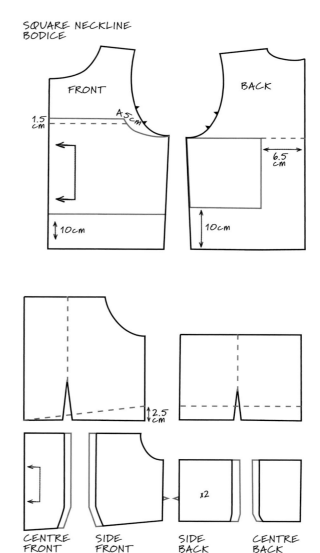

PATTERN PIECES

DENIM FABRIC
- ☐ 1x centre front (on fold)
- ☐ 2x side front
- ☐ 2x centre back
- ☐ 2x side back
- ☐ 2x straps
- ☐ 1x tie

LINING
- ☐ 1x centre front (on fold)
- ☐ 2x side front
- ☐ 2x centre back
- ☐ 2x side back

- ☐ 1x bias binding

CENTRE FRONT

SIDE FRONT

SIDE BACK

CENTRE BACK

STRAP

TIE

BIAS BINDING

SEWING THE TOP

(1)   (2)

(6)

(7)

(8)

1. For both outer and lining tops, sew centre front to side front, right sides together. Press seam open and clip if needed to lie flat

2. For both outer and lining tops, sew centre back to side back, right sides together. Press seam open and clip if needed to lie flat

3. Sew front and back pieces together at side seams, right sides together, and press seams open

4. Stay stitch armholes

5. Draw a line with chalk through the centre front of the top

6. On the outer top, pin ribbon/binding (binding channel) onto the inside of the seams you have just sewn, pinning straight through the middle of the seam.

> *Note:* You can choose to complete steps 6–11 on lining bodice if you would prefer channel stitches to be hidden on your finished garment. Continue with project as normal.

7. Turn the top to the right side and transfer pins to the right side, ensuring the pins are through the middle of the seams or chalk lines. Make sure the channel remains in the middle too. You can baste these down if you want

8. From the right side, topstitch all channels on with two lines of stitching, 6mm away from seam/chalk line at either side

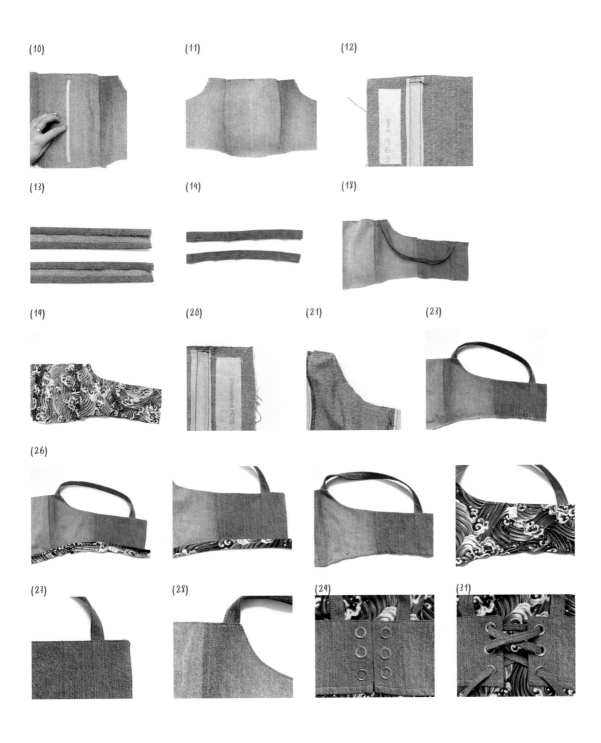

9. Stitch across only the top of channels at 1cm
10. Measure the length of boning you need for each seam. Remove 1.5cm length from top edge and 2cm from bottom edge for seam allowances.
11. Cut boning lengths and prepare the ends of the boning. Insert boning into channel and stitch across bottom of channels at 1cm
12. Interface centre back section to reinforce where eyelets will be placed. Use a small rectangle of fabric that sits 1.5cm away from all edges.
13. Create straps by pressing long edges in by 1cm
14. Press in half lengthways
15. Topstitch along both long edges of strap
16. Pin straps into place on outer bodice. Back of strap should sit at seam of side back and centre back. Front strap should sit at corner of side front, 1.5cm away from armhole edge
17. Try bodice on and adjust length of strap as needed
18. Stitch in place at 1cm
19. Pin lining bodice on top of outer bodice, right sides together
20. Sew around these two layers, along centre back edge, armhole, and front neck edge
21. Trim and clip seam allowance
22. Turn to right side, press and under-stitch lining where possible
23. Press whole edge
24. Baste bottom edge of top to secure outer and lining layer together, at 7mm
25. Create length of bias binding (see "Build from the Basics" (page 40) for instructions) from lining fabric
26. Sew this onto bottom edge, using method to conceal binding
27. When stitching bias binding down in final step, use topstitching thread if you have used it throughout the rest of the project. If you have concealed your boning on the lining fabric, hand stitch the bias binding to the lining to prevent visible stitching
28. Topstitch around rest of bodice edge if desired
29. Insert eyelets at centre back, ensuring they are evenly spaced apart
30. Create ties by folding short end in by 1cm. Fold long edges in by 1cm on either side. Fold in half along long edge. Topstitch closed
31. Thread ties through eyelets

A note on eyelets : there are a couple of different types of eyelets than can be used in sewing - including metal or hand-sewn ones. I prefer using metal eyelets for ease and time reasons. These are easily found online or in craft stores, and always come with instructions on how to insert them. I recommend practising inserting a few before you try on your garment.

THE
EVERYDAY ROBE

FIRST THINGS FIRST

A dressing gown is a great project for taking the drop shoulder bodice block a few steps further. It is also a fantastic project to make as a present for someone, since it doesn't need fitting and adjustments. Although I've called this project The Everyday Robe, you can use more exuberant and luxurious fabrics for your dressing gown for a fancier feel, or stick to a good quality cotton lawn for a light and summery soft feel. You could even use towelling or fluffy fabric to make a classic cosier dressing gown. Use a fabric design that you wouldn't normally sew or wear, since you'll only be wearing it around the house anyway! Lemons and dalmatians aren't a combination you frequently see together, but in a dressing gown, somehow it works.

Patterns needed: bodice block, sleeve block

Techniques learned: patch pockets

Seam allowances: 1.5cm unless otherwise stated

NOTION LIST:
- Matching thread
- Interfacing for neck facing and belt

MAKING THE PATTERN

This dressing gown pattern is made from the drop shoulder bodice created on page 52. So, if you haven't got that made already, create that and then we will make some more adjustments to create a dressing gown pattern. Pattern measurements already contain seam allowances.

FRONT

1. Cut bodice down centre front
2. Extend waist width by 12cm and grade this to meet shoulder
3. Extend bodice to length you desire; I added 85.5cm (including hem allowance of 3cm) to make ankle length
4. Extend armhole by 2.5cm and continue this down whole bodice side seam – adding extra as needed to make the side seam and the hem meet at a right angle

MAKE NOTCHES FOR YOUR BELT LOOPS:
- One 2cm above the waistline of your bodice
- Other one 8cm below the first

MAKE PATTERN MARKINGS FOR YOUR POCKET PLACEMENT:
- Should be parallel to your side seam, about 10cm in from edge of pattern piece
- Should sit around hip level, top of pocket piece (unsewn) 10cm from waistline of original bodice

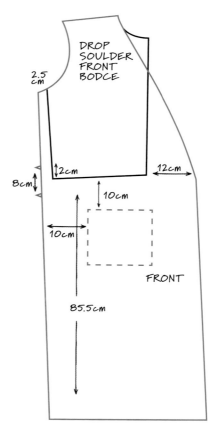

BACK

1. Extend bodice to length you desire, I added 85.5cm (including hem allowance of 3cm) to make ankle length
2. Extend armhole by 2.5cm and continue this down whole bodice side seam
3. Add 2.5cm at centre back and continue this down whole bodice side seam, adding extra as needed to make the side seam and the hem form a right angle when they meet

SLEEVE

1. Use full length sleeve pattern
2. Extend armhole curve by 2.5cm at either side and continue this down whole sleeve piece

TIE

14cm x 100cm (make longer as needed and use an existing tie as a reference)

POCKETS

23 cm x 24.5 cm

BELT LOOPS

4 cm x 10 cm

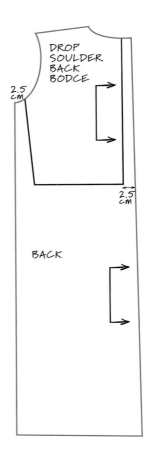

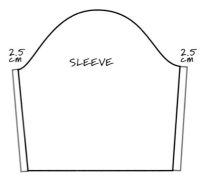

HANGING LOOP (SAME AS BELT LOOP)

4 cm x 10 cm

NECK FACING

- 14cm wide
- Length of neck facing will depend on how long your dressing gown will be
- It should be the length of the front neck edge x2 plus the length of the back neck edge, adding on 1.5cm seam allowance at hem and wherever you need to seam rectangles together to obtain length (mine was 306cm long)

PATTERN PIECES

- ☐ 2x front
- ☐ 1x back (on fold)
- ☐ 2x sleeve
- ☐ 1x neck facing (made from as many rectangles as needed)*
  - ☐ Plus interfacing
- ☐ 1x tie (made from as many rectangles as needed)*
  - ☐ Plus interfacing
- ☐ 2x pocket*
- ☐ 2x belt loop*
- ☐ 1x hanging loop*

*These items were cut from a different fabric to the body

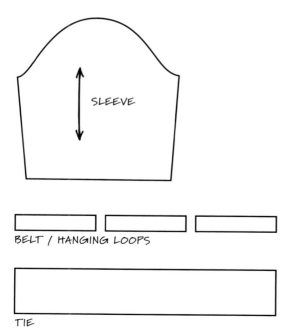

SLEEVE

BELT / HANGING LOOPS

TIE

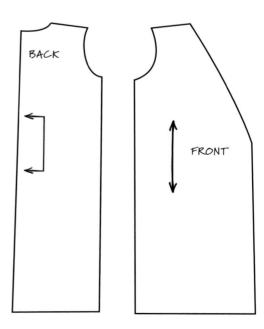

BACK

FRONT

SEWING THE DRESSING GOWN

THE POCKET

1. Press top of pockets in 1cm
2. Fold the top down 2cm towards the front of the pocket, i.e., with right sides of fabric together and pin at the edges – don't press this
3. Stitch at 1.5cm at either side of the fold
4. Finish other three edges of pocket
5. Turn top of pocket to the right side, pressing out the corners so they are sharp, the two sides of the pocket should now fold in by 1.5cm
6. Press the sides and bottom of the pocket in by 1.5cm
7. Stitch across top of pocket, a few mm away from folded edge
8. Pin pockets in place on dressing gown and topstitch down around three bottom edges

THE BODY

9. Sew front to back at shoulder seams, right sides together, finish seam allowances and press open
10. Sew sleeve into armhole, right sides together, following notches, finish seam allowances and press to sleeve
11. Sew side seams, right sides together, finish seam allowances and press open
12. Sew sleeve hems by pressing in 1cm and pressing in 2cm again. Stitch close to folded edge
13. Hem dressing gown by pressing in

(1)
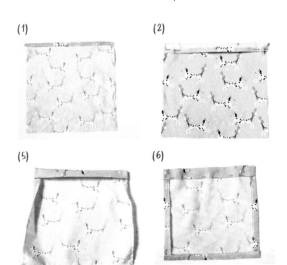

(2)

(4)
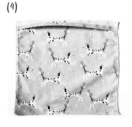

(5)

(6)

(8)
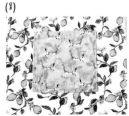

1cm and pressing in 2cm again. Stitch close to folded edge

14. Create hanging loop by folding fabric in half lengthways, right sides together
15. Sew along long edge
16. Press seam open in middle of loop, trim seam allowances

17. Turn to right side
18. Press flat with seam in middle of loop
19. Pin this at the wrong side of centre back neckline with the short ends about 5cm apart to create a hanging loop

THE NECK FACING

20. Stitch together rectangles to create a neck facing long enough, press seams open
21. Interface one long side of the facing
22. Fold the facing piece in half, wrong sides together and press
23. On the non-interfaced side, press the raw edge in by 1cm
24. Pin the interfaced side of the facing around the neckline of the dressing gown, making sure you have at least 1cm of overhang at either side of the hem
25. Sew around this edge
26. Trim seam allowance and press towards facing
27. Fold the short edges of the facing back on itself so the fabric is right sides together, folding along the middle fold you initially created. You should have a slight overhang of fabric on the non-interfaced side of the facing

(19)

(23)

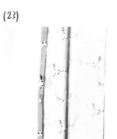

(24)

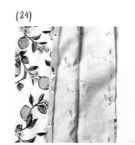

(26)

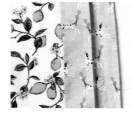

(27)

28. Stitch a line straight across, at the level of the dressing gown hem
29. Trim any excess fabric down to 7mm
30. Turn facing right side out and you should see that the overhang of facing on the inside covers the facing seam.
31. From the right side, pin the facing seam, catching the excess facing

fabric on the inside
32. Stitch in the ditch the whole way around the neckline, ensuring you catch the free edge of the facing in your stitches – this means you are sewing on the line of the existing seam. Do this slowly to make it nice and neat

THE BELT

33. Create tie by folding in half right sides together along long edge
34. Sew around short ends and long edge of tie, leaving 8cm gap in middle unsewn – make pointy ends if you want; see "Build from the Basics" (page 29) to learn how
35. Trim and clip seam allowances
36. Turn to right side through gap
37. Press tie flat and close gap either with hand sewing or topstitching around whole of tie

38. Create belt loops by folding fabric in half long ways
39. Sew along long edge
40. Press seam open in middle of loop, trim seam allowances
41. Turn to right side
42. Press flat with seam in middle of loop
43. Sew belt loops to side seams of dressing gown at your waist. Fold each short edge of the belt loop in by 1cm and topstitch down across short end at either side of loop

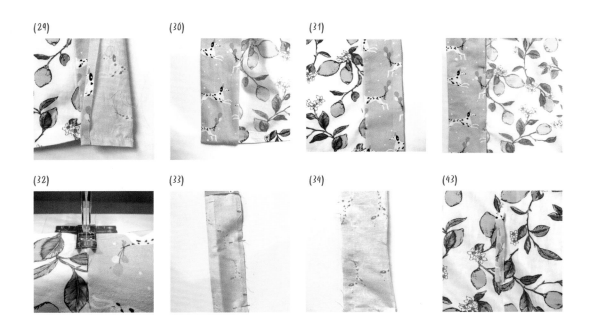

(29)   (30)   (31)

(32)   (33)   (34)   (43)

GLOSSARY

BODICE
The upper part of a garment, covering the front and back of the chest above the waist, and excluding the sleeves.

PATTERN BLOCK
A foundation pattern that can be used as a base to create designs.

PATTERN PIECE
A template that is used as a guide for cutting out pieces of fabric for a garment.

PLACKET
An opening on a garment where it fastens or where there is a pocket.

RIGHT SIDE AND WRONG SIDE
The right side of the fabric is the one that will sit on the outside of the garment; this may be patterned or have a texture. The wrong side of the fabric will sit on the inside of the garment.

SEAM ALLOWANCE
The area between the edge of the fabric and the stitching line. The width of the seam allowance may vary.

STITCH IN THE DITCH
Sewing along a seamline from the right side, after the seam has been sewn.

TOILE
An early version of a garment made using cheaper materials, allowing the fit and design to be perfected.

YOKE
The part of a garment that sits at the shoulders, to which the main body of the garment is attached.

ENDNOTE

I hope that by the time you reach this point, you have made some incredible clothes and are eager to explore sewing even more! Please continue learning and enjoying this wonderful craft and send me pictures of anything you've made from these project pages, I would absolutely love to see them. The best place to find me is on Instagram. Thank you again for picking up this creation of mine. It is truly astounding to me that I have had this opportunity.

@serenasews_   #SerenaSews